# Forewor

The iPhone 6 is Apple's biggest ever phone. And the iPhone 6 Plus is even bigger. Since they already have big sales to match, it's fair to say Apple has found a new way to make its industry-leading devices even more desirable.

The iPhone 6 series epitomises Apple's approach to product design. Even smarter technology is packed into an even slimmer and more perfectly engineered case. Nothing is just for show: it's all to enhance the way your iPhone feels and what it can do for you. This guide shares the same intent, so read on and get more from your iPhone 6 with iOS 8.

### Adam Banks
Editor in Chief, MacUser

 @macusermagazine

# Contents

## 1 The hardware
p6

## 2 Setting up
p28

## 6 Accessories

**Choose practical and stylish add-ons for your iPhone 6 from Apple and third-party manufacturers**

# 3 iOS 8 p42

# 4 iTunes and iCloud p104

# 5 Apps p124

# Chapter 1
# The hardware

# iPhone 6

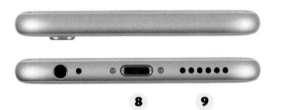

### ⑥ Apps
Around a million apps are available for iOS, the iPhone's mobile operating system.

### ① iSight camera
The iPhone 6's new rear camera features 'focus pixels' for fast autofocus via phase detection. As well as 8 megapixel stills and up to 43 megapixel panaroramas, it can shoot 1080p Full HD up to 240 frames per second for 8× slow motion. The dual LED True Tone flash complements the natural lighting of your scene.

### ③ Aluminium back
Anodised in Silver, Space Grey or Gold, the case curves at the edges to meet the front, with no sides. The Apple logo is inset in stainless steel.

### ④ FaceTime camera
The front camera is 720p HD for FaceTime, Skype and selfies. Face recognition and automatic HDR help ensure a clear image.

### ⑦ Touch ID
Optional fingerprint recognition lets you unlock your phone with a touch. It also acts as a security barrier for buying apps and music, paying with your iPhone and more.

### ⑧ Lightning port
The iPhone has just one charging and accessory interface, the ultra-compact Lightning connector.

### ② Wireless stripes
Where the iPhone 5 series had plastic panels in its metal back to let the various radio signals in and out, the iPhone 6 just has these narrow rubber strips at the top and bottom.

### ⑤ Retina display
At 1334 × 750 pixels, the 4.7-inch screen is bigger than previous iPhones and has a higher 1400:1 contrast ratio, so it looks vivid and sharp. The glass curves at the edges.

### ⑨ Audio
There's a general purpose speaker on the bottom edge as well as one at the top for when you're on the phone. There are also three mics, including one on the left here.

# iPhone 6 Plus

**❶ Rounded edges**

Both the iPhone 6 and the 6 Plus have curved edges, with the front glass rounded off to meet the aluminium back at an almost undetectable seam. There are no 'sides'.

**The iPhone 6 is 138.1mm tall (shown on p8 at actual size), 67.0mm wide and just 6.9mm thick. It weighs 129 grams, slightly more than the iPhone 5s. The iPhone 6 Plus is 158.1mm tall (shown opposite at actual size), 77.8mm wide and 7.1mm thick, 5mm thinner than the iPhone 5s. It weighs 172 grams.**

**❷ Retina display**

The iPhone 6 Plus has a 1920 × 1080 pixel (Full HD) 5.5-inch screen, the biggest ever on an iPhone. It packs in more pixels per inch than the iPhone 5 series for an even sharper image, and its 1300:1 contrast ratio is 60% higher. If your thumb can't reach the top of the screen, tap the Touch ID button twice and the display slides down to meet you.

**❸ iSight camera**

The iPhone 6 Plus is the first iPhone to provide optical image stabilisation, helping to avoid camera shake, especially in low light.

**❹ True Tone flash**

As on other smartphones, the iPhone's 'flash' is a continuous light source, so you can use it for video as well as photos – or as a torch. It contains two different colours of LED lamp, and the iPhone's software illuminates these in the best proportions to match the lighting it detects in the scene you're photographing. This creates more natural-looking results than standard flash.

**❺ Aluminium back**

This metal's properties allow Apple to build a very thin case that's still strong and resistant to scratching.

# Buttons

**❶ Home**

Originally marked with a round-cornered square, the iPhone's main button is now blank because it houses the Touch ID fingerprint scanner. When your iPhone is showing the Lock screen (as seen here), press the Home or Sleep button to wake it, then touch Home to unlock it to the Home screen (as seen on previous page).

**Hold down the Sleep button to turn the iPhone off (this is rarely necessary); hold it again to turn it back on. Or hold Sleep and Home together to reset it.**

## ❷ Sleep

This button, previously on the top, is now on the right. Press it and let go to put the iPhone to sleep, so that you don't accidentally touch anything.

### ❸ Silent

Flip this toggle switch towards the back of the iPhone to turn off the ringer. It reveals a small orange line to show it's off, and a crossed-out speaker icon briefly appears on the screen to confirm.

### ❹ Volume

These plus and minus buttons control the level of whatever audio is playing, subject to your choices in Settings. You can also press one of them in the Camera app to take a picture – hold the iPhone sideways with the buttons at the top. The volume buttons on your EarPods also do this.

iPhone

Designed by Apple in California  Assembled in China  Model A1586
FCC: X1 BCG-E3816A  IC:579C-E2816A  IMEI: 352067062978427

# Sound

### FaceTime microphone

A third microphone, hidden behind the front panel, picks up your voice when you're using the front camera.

### Earpiece

This speaker is used only when your iPhone is held against your ear for phone calls. Tap the speaker icon on screen to switch to the bottom speaker (see right) and make the caller audible to people around you.

### Voice microphone

This small hole on the left of the bottom edge is for the microphone that picks up your voice when you're holding the iPhone to your ear. It's also used for audio recording, so aim your voice, musical instrument or whatever at this when capturing sounds in apps.

### Speaker

The grille on the right is the iPhone's main speaker. It's surprisingly powerful for such a tiny component – handy for listening to the radio or playing games. You may hear a bit of distortion at maximum volume.

### Video microphone

On the back of the iPhone, between the iSight camera and flash, is a second microphone to pick up sound from in front of you when you're shooting video.

# Audio output

### Control Center

Available at any time by swiping up steadily from the bottom of the screen, this lets you adjust the volume of any audio that's currently playing, among many other features.

### Bluetooth

The industry standard wireless format is supported for audio and other accessories. You can turn it on and off here, but you have to go to Settings > Bluetooth to add new devices.

### Headphone

This is a standard analogue 3.5mm socket, so you can attach any headphones or accessories or use an audio cable to connect a speaker or hifi system. It supports three-ring plugs for headsets with mics and inline remote clickers, which can control volume and answer and end calls.

### AirPlay

Apple's AirPlay works over wifi and makes it easy to direct audio or video output to accessories. Tap here, then pick the device to send to.

# EarPods

Your iPhone comes with these excellent Apple earphones as standard. The way they fit into your ears is different from other models, cleverly directing the sound forward into your ear canal rather than perpendicular to your head. They don't block out all external sounds, which makes them safer to wear outdoors, but they provide enough isolation to let you enjoy whatever you're listening to in most environments.

**Easy fit**
Apple's ergonomic earpieces sit securely but not tightly in your ears, making them comfortable for most people to use.

**Remote**
Built into the cable for the right earpiece is this remote clicker. Squeeze the central depressed area to play or pause a track or to answer or end a phone call. The plus and minus buttons control volume.

# Lightning

Apple was criticised for replacing the iOS 30-pin connector with a brand new proprietary design back when it introduced the iPhone 5. But the Lightning port is by far the best connector around. The tiny, sturdy plug has no sharp edges and fits in either way, so it's no hassle to plug in the supplied charging cable (right) or any other compatible accessory. All current iPhones and iPads use Lightning – although it now has a rival in the similar-sized USB Type-C.

**Lightning plug**
The eight contacts are duplicated on both sides, so it doesn't matter which way round you insert it.

**30-pin adaptor**
Buy an adaptor like this to use most accessories made for Apple's bigger 30-pin connector. Video functions, however, won't work.

# Retina display

**Closer to real** Apple uses the term 'Retina' to describe screens that have so many pixels, the human eye can't resolve them at a typical viewing distance, so you're not aware that the image is made up of individual dots. Every Retina iPhone has had a pixel density of 326ppi except the 6 Plus, at 401ppi.

The sense of reality is further enhanced by graphical features of iOS 8. On the Home screen, the background, icons and text labels are all contained in separate layers which move independently as you tilt the iPhone in your hand. This creates a parallax effect, as if the background is behind the screen and the icons on the surface. It's a subtle enhancement, but if you find it too distracting you can remove the effect: open the Settings app, tap General then Accessibility, and turn on Reduce Motion.

Powerful backlighting means the iPhone screen has a very high maximum brightness. You can adjust the level from Control Center (see p50) or in Settings > Wallpaper & Brightness, where you can also turn Auto-Brightness on or off. Auto-Brightness still respects your chosen setting, but uses the iPhone's ambient light sensor to adjust it as the light level around you varies, to give you the same perceived brightness.

The iPhone also has a proximity sensor that detects when you hold it up to your face to take a phone call and turns off the screen.

# Cameras

**iSight** The iPhone's rear-facing camera, which Apple brands as 'iSight', keeps getting even better. While the 8 megapixel resolution matches previous models, the iPhone 6 has a new trick: phase detect autofocus, which Apple calls 'focus pixels'. The result is especially noticeable when shooting video: whatever you point at quickly and smoothly comes into focus without having to stop. You can shoot a standard 30 or a super-real 60 frames per second in 1080p HD, or up to 240fps at 720p for 8× slow motion. The iPhone 6 Plus adds optical image stabilisation to counteract small amounts of camera shake. Both phones have quite effective software stabilisation for shaky video.

**FaceTime** The 720p camera on the front of the iPhone, for video chat and selfies, has enhanced face recognition and low-light performance keep the picture clear.

**Lens**
Five glass elements help you get great shots

# True Tone flash

**Natural colour** The LED light on the back of the iPhone was always useful when shooting in low light. Although Apple calls it a 'flash', it gives continuous light, so you can use it for video as well as stills. Since the iPhone 5s, there are actually two LED lamps behind a ridged lens, one warm and one cool in colour temperature. These fire in proportion to mimic the ambient light where you're shooting. This technique, which Apple calles True Tone, avoids the sickly glare that you often get from a built-in flash, especially with LEDs, which tend to generate a narrow range of frequencies. Instead, photos come out looking bright but natural. You can help things along by standing fairly close but not *too* close to the subject.

# Inside the iPhone 6

### Barrier to entry

The way into the iPhone is by removing the screen with a suction cup – or even better, iFixit's iSclack (from eustore.ifixit.com). But care is required to avoid damaging delicate connections.

## Battery

Apple doesn't design this to be removable, so replacing it if it wears out is not really a DIY job, although it's doable.

Li-Ion Polymer Battery
3.82V ⎓ 11.1 Wh
APN: 616-0772

⚠ WARNING
Authorized Service Provider Only

## Logic board

Nearly all of the iPhone's electronics are crammed into this strip of circuit board along the right-hand side. The rest of the ultra-slim case is taken up by the battery.

PHOTOS COURTESY OF IFIXIT.COM

# Parts

### iSight camera

The iPhone 6 Plus (inset) gains electromagnets to move the lens in response to data from the accelerometer and gyroscope, counteracting camera shake. The 4.7in iPhone 6 (main picture) doesn't have this feature.

### Touch ID

Tweaks to the fingerprint recognition components make it faster and more reliable than before.

## Repairability

The iPhone 6 and 6 Plus have both been rated a respectable 7 out of 10 for repairability by iFixit.com.

## Wifi

The iPhone 6 supports the latest 802.11ac protocol for fast wifi.

## SIM

This tray pops out with a supplied tool and takes a nano-SIM, the smallest type.

## Glue

There's less than in previous models, but the battery is still stuck in.

PHOTOS COURTESY OF IFIXIT.COM

## Mobile networking

Antennas built into the case can connect to a variety of cell bands. All UK networks are supported, including the new 4G services, and you can use your iPhone unmodified in almost any other country too.

# The A8

**Speed king**

To keep the iPhone ahead of the game, Apple designs its own 'system in package' chips to squeeze the maximum amount of processing power into the space available. The latest, the A8, continues the trend. Seen here mounted on the 4.7in iPhone 6's main logic board, it's a 64-bit computer containing more than two billion transistors. CPU and GPU (central processor and graphics processor) components are built in, along with the M8 motion coprocessor, which lets your iPhone track your movements constantly in the background – invaluable data for health and fitness apps. The A8 also handles dedicated image processing tasks that enable the advanced features of the iSight camera.

Apple claims the A8 doubles the CPU performance of the iPhone 5s's A7 and offers up to 84% more graphics speed. Just as importantly, it's 50% more energy-efficient, so despite doing even more work the iPhone 6 has longer, not shorter, battery life.

PHOTO COURTESY OF IFIXIT.COM

# Touch ID

**For your eyes only** Setting your phone to lock itself when idle keeps the contents safe from prying eyes if you leave it lying around or have it stolen. *Really* safe, because your data is encrypted. The weakest link is the passcode you type in to unlock, which could be guessed. So Apple has built in a fingerprint scanner. When you set up your new iPhone, you're invited to register one or more fingerprints. A longish touch on the Home button will then unlock your phone. Apple is keenly aware of security, and says fingerprint data is only stored, encrypted, on the A8 chip, never sent over the internet. If you'd still prefer to use your passcode, you can; and either way you'll need to enter your passcode periodically for security, so don't forget it.

*9:41 AM*     *100%*

*Complete*

Touch ID is ready. Your print can be used for unlocking your iPhone.

*Continue*

# Chapter 2
# Setting up

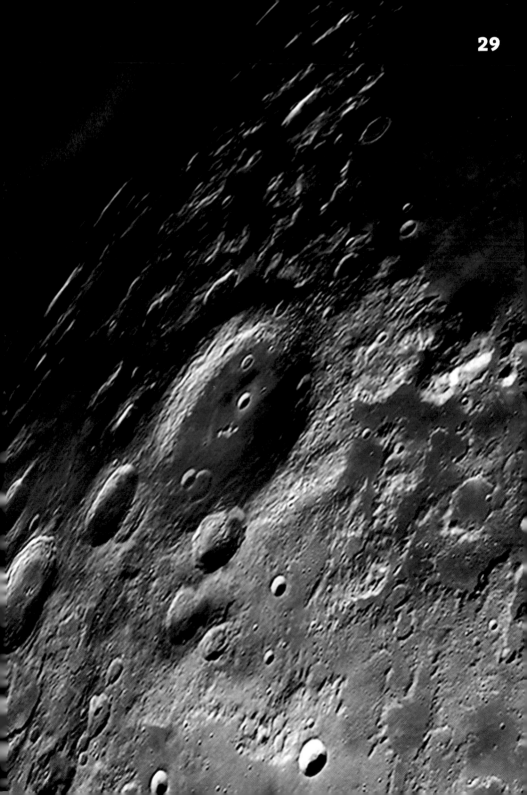

# Connecting

**Inserting your SIM**

Every mobile phone needs a SIM card to identify it to the network you use. If you bought your iPhone (or got it as an upgrade) on contract, a nano-SIM will have been provided. If you bought it outright from Apple, and your previous phone used a micro- or mini-SIM, you'll need to ask your chosen mobile network to send you a replacement nano-SIM.

Clipped into the paperwork in the top of your iPhone's box is a loop-shaped metal SIM ejector tool. Insert it into the small hole on the right side of the iPhone and press firmly to eject the SIM tray. Pull this all the way out and fit the SIM into it, taking care that its orientation matches the markings. Be sure you've got this right, or the tray could get stuck in your iPhone. Now reinsert the tray, and make sure it's all the way in.

Turn on the iPhone by pressing the Home button and run through the setup steps that appear. (See p34 if you've had an iPhone before and want to install the same content on the new one.) After you choose a language, it'll need to connect to the internet to activate itself with Apple's server. At this point you can either connect to a wifi network where you are, or tap Use Mobile Connection to get online via your mobile tariff.

**Data usage**

When you reach the iPhone's Home screen, tap the Settings icon and then tap Mobile in the first group of options. Mobile Data refers to web pages, emails, music downloads and any other kind of data when you access it over the mobile network, as opposed to via wifi. You may not be aware of using it, since your iPhone will refresh data in some apps automatically, and actions such as playing a music track that's stored in the cloud will

← **Accessing the internet over a mobile connection uses up your data allowance. In Settings you can control and monitor how much you use.**

initiate downloads. Most mobile tariffs have a monthly data limit, beyond which you'll pay extra, so you'll want to use wifi instead for tasks that use a lot of data, such as streaming video from YouTube. When your iPhone is connected to a wifi network, it won't use any mobile data.

If you take your iPhone abroad, your network will charge much higher data fees, by the megabyte. As many users have found, these 'roaming' charges can get very expensive very quickly, resulting in bills tens of times higher than usual at the end of the month. If your SIM is from a network within the EU (including the UK) and you travel within the EU, roaming charges are now lower thanks to new regulations. Elsewhere, they can be astronomical. Turning off Data Roaming right now will avoid any surprises if you go abroad in future.

Later in this guide you'll see how to control exactly what your iPhone uses mobile data for. If you're concerned about using up your data allowance before you get around to adjusting these settings, you could turn off Mobile Data for now as well. You'll still be able to connect via wifi.

Lower down the Mobile Settings page, you can check your mobile data usage. But many networks provide their own app to do this more effectively. Search for it in the App Store or ask your network for details.

## Connecting via wifi

Tap Wi-Fi at the top of the Settings app to connect to a wifi network. The first switch here turns wifi on and off, but you can do that more conveniently in Control Centre (see p50). The reason to come to Settings is to choose which network to connect to. Wait for the list of nearby networks to finish populating. If the one you want doesn't appear, it may be set not to broadcast its name; tap Other… and enter its details. Otherwise, just tap any of the networks listed. Most networks show a padlock and will require a password.

Once you connect to any network, iOS remembers it and reconnects to it when in range. So whenever you're at home, at work, or anywhere you've used wifi before, you're automatically connected. If you want to stop using a network, or its password changes, tap the 'i' to its right, then Forget this Network. In the same place, you can enter technical details a corporate network might require.

If there's no network nearby that you've used before, but one you haven't, iOS will ask if you want to join it. If this gets annoying, turn off Ask to Join Networks.

Many public wifi hotspots require you to log in on each use. A web page for this should pop up when you join the network, but if not, open Safari and try to go to any web page. This should kick the registration page into action.

**↓ As long as wifi is turned on, your iPhone will connect to wifi wherever you have before.**

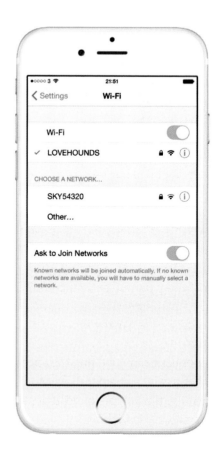

# Charging

When you connect your iPhone to an electrical supply, whether through a mains adaptor or a powered USB port on a computer, a chime indicates that it's receiving power. If you don't hear it, check the power adaptor and cable or ensure that the USB port you're using is capable of providing power. A visual charge indicator always appears at the top right of the screen; the Battery Percentage option in Settings > General > Usage makes this more precise. Tap Battery Usage here to see which apps have used the most power in the last day and week.

Tasks such as games will drain the battery more quickly. Background App Refresh (p56) is designed to minimise use of the power-hungry mobile data connection, but limiting the apps that use it can help further. More battery tips can be found at apple.com/batteries/iphone.

**↓ On plugging your iPhone in, you should hear a soft chime and briefly see this graphic.**

# Restoring

If you've owned an iPhone (or iPad or iPod touch) before, you can easily transfer its apps, data and settings to your new iPhone from a backup.

Any iOS device can be constantly backed up to iCloud, so your data is safe if it gets damaged, lost or stolen. You can alternatively back it up to a Mac or PC via iTunes, but using iCloud is much simpler. Once set up, the backup will be updated daily when your iPhone is plugged into an electrical supply and connected via wifi. You can restore your backup at any time to the same device, if you have problems, or to a new device.

Ensure you're signed in with your Apple ID in Settings, under iCloud in the fourth group down. (For information about Apple ID, see support.apple.com/kb/ HT4895.) On the device to back up, go to Settings and tap General in the third group down, and then Usage. You can see how much of your free 5GB iCloud allowance is in use. Apps and iTunes purchases don't count – only personal data

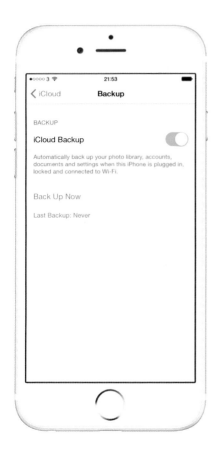

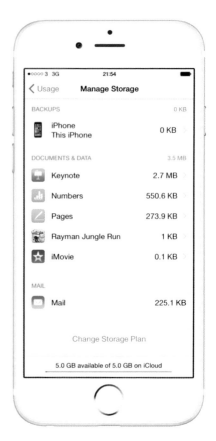

**← You can set up your iPhone with the same content you had on a previous Apple device.**

**↑ Turn on iCloud Backup and tap Back Up Now to copy all your data to iCloud. It'll update the backup later automatically.**

**↗ Tap Manage Storage to check how much iCloud space is free.**

such as photos will use up this space. Turn on iCloud Backup and backups start automatically.

When you activate your new iPhone, ensure it's on wifi, then opt to Restore from iCloud. Pick the backup of your old device. It'll take a while to restore everything, but you can still use the phone.

Turn on iCloud Backup to keep your new iPhone backed up too.

# Tethering

**Connect other devices via your iPhone**

The Personal Hotspot feature enables you to share your iPhone's cellular network connection with an iPad, Mac, game console or other device that doesn't have its own mobile tariff. Once you turn your iPhone into a Personal Hotspot, you can 'tether' devices to it over Bluetooth, wifi or USB.

Before you use Personal Hotspot, check with your mobile network whether your tariff allows tethering and if it will incur extra charges. If you plan to use it regularly, you may be able to change your tariff so that you pay a more reasonable extra monthly fee for tethering up to a data limit, rather than running up charges per megabyte each time you use it.

To turn on Personal Hotspot for the first time, open the Settings app and tap Mobile at the top, then tap Personal Hotspot and flick the switch to turn it on. From then on, a shortcut to Personal Hotspot will appear alongside Mobile at the top of the Settings app.

If both wifi and Bluetooth are turned off when you switch on Personal Hotspot, you'll be asked whether you want to turn them on, or alternatively if you'll only tether to a Mac or PC via USB. Personal Hotspot can be left enabled all the time, but you might want to turn it off to ensure other devices that automatically download updates don't do so unexpectedly via your iPhone, eating up your tethered data allowance.

While any device is connected (not when Personal Hotspot is turned on but idle), the status bar at the top of your iPhone's screen will double in height to accommodate information about your Personal Hotspot activity. When your Personal Hotspot is active, other devices can connect via wifi, Bluetooth or USB in the same way they would to any hotspot;

**← Personal Hotspot has only two settings: on (green) or off, and the password for other devices to connect over wifi. If devices are connected, the top bar turns blue and counts them.**

see their own documentation for instructions. It's even simpler from a Mac running OS X 10.10 Yosemite: your iPhone automatically appears as a wifi network.

If a wireless device can't connect, go to the Personal Hotspot page in Settings and leave it open while you connect. It should work fine then, even if you leave the Settings app, but you may need to repeat this technique when re-establishing the connection later.

Personal Hotspot allows up to five devices to connect at once. If one of these is a Mac or PC, however, you can use its own Internet Sharing (Mac) or Internet Connection Sharing (Windows) feature to share with more devices. Connect the computer to your iPhone using your Lightning to USB cable. On a Mac, open System Preferences, go to Sharing and make sure it's unlocked (bottom left). Select Internet Sharing on the left, then set 'Share your connection from' to iPhone USB. Below, tick Wi-Fi, then click Wi-Fi Options to name your network and set up a password. Finally, tick the box next to Internet Sharing and click Start in the confirmation pane.

In Windows, setting this up differs between versions. For Windows Vista and 7, see tinyurl.com/oxo5ymc. Windows 8 makes it rather complicated; the free utility Virtual Router can help (virtualrouter.codeplex.com).

# Alert sounds

iOS includes a range of beautifully produced sounds that you can assign to various events, such as calendar alerts, reminders and new messages, as well as to your phone ringtone. Assign a default ringtone in the Settings app under Sounds > Sounds and Vibration Patterns. You can even compose your own vibration pattern.

These settings can be overridden for specific people in the Contacts app. Tap a person's name, then Edit at the top right, then the Ringtone row, and pick a different sound. Adjacent to that, you can set a vibration pattern to identify callers when your iPhone is in your pocket. Further down, you can create a pattern, or disable vibrations for that person.

The link at the top of the sound list takes you to ringtones on the iTunes Store. Alternatively, you can make your own using Apple's GarageBand app (p127).

**↓ Assigned sounds not only get your attention, but let you know what's going on.**

**Do Not Disturb**

When you don't want sounds to interrupt you, get some peace and quiet by turning on Do Not Disturb. A smarter version of silent mode, this blocks incoming calls and alerts, but alarms in the Clock app will still wake you. It works in two ways. You can turn it on at any time by tapping the moon icon in the top row of Control Center (see p50). When Do Not Disturb is on, a moon icon appears among the icons in the status bar.

**↓ Do Not Disturb can be scheduled to minimise interruptions to sleep or work.**

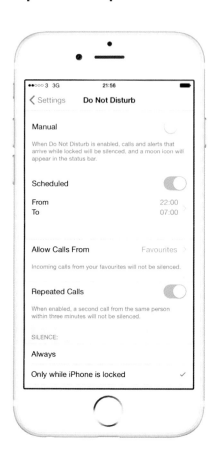

(The switch labelled 'Manually' in the Do Not Disturb page of Settings has the same effect.)

Alternatively, you can schedule Do Not Disturb to activate between certain times. Only one such period can be set, so you'll need to manually turn it on at any additional times you need it.

Not all calls have to be blocked. The Repeated Calls switch allows a determined caller to reach you if they try twice within three minutes when Do Not Disturb is on. Even with this disabled, you can allow calls from a specified group to get through. Tap the 'Allow Calls From' option and choose Favorites (your Favorites are managed in the Phone app) or another group that you've created (via icloud.com in a web browser on a Mac or PC).

If you choose No One here, and disallow repeated calls, no calls or alerts will interrupt you until Do Not Disturb is turned off.

# Privacy

***Keep it to yourself***

With so much personal information on your iPhone, and a connection to the internet often available, you might have concerns about what apps could do by putting these things together. Whether or not the NSA or GCHQ is interested in you, marketing and advertising companies certainly are, including giants like Google and Facebook that harvest data on users of their free services for the benefit of their paying clients.

Apple prefers to sell products to users, and has an interest in making you feel safe. iOS doesn't allow open access to your location, contacts or calendars; apps need your permission to use them. Look under Privacy in the Settings app to see what you can restrict access to ❶. The first group contains hardware features and apps whose data other apps can ask to access. Tap an item to see which apps have requested access to it.

Even if you've granted access previously, it can be revoked. For example, if you've decided you don't want your home location attached to tweets, tap Location Services followed by Twitter, and then choose Never.

Further down the Privacy page you'll find your Facebook and Twitter accounts. Tap to see which services can access them. What they're doing with that access might be unclear, but you can guess. Facebook's access to Photos is to allow you to post photos from your Camera Roll, innocuously enough. Games tend to use your Facebook account to start multiplayer matches with your friends (although this is really Game Center's job). If in doubt, check the app's website or App Store page for a privacy policy. The decision to allow access is yours, based on who you trust.

Apple does operate iAds, which allows apps to display ads that are tailored to your interests based on activity on your device (although this

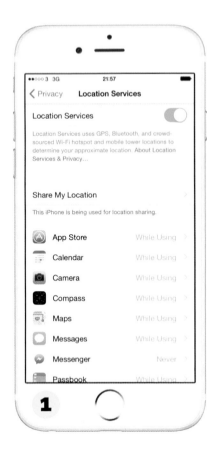

is never linked to your actual identity). Turning on Limit Ad Tracking, under Advertising, stops your data being used to target these ads, but it doesn't stop you seeing ads.

Safari's settings include a Do Not Track option, part of a broader industry initiative to request that websites don't record your visit. It's up to websites to honour this: see donottrack.us.

**↑ The idea of being tracked electronically may not appeal, but if you lose your iPhone you'll wish it could be. And it can. In Settings > iCloud, turn on Find My iPhone and its Send Last Location option. Sign into the Find My iPhone app on any iOS device, or at icloud.com on a computer, to trace or disable this phone in future.**

# Chapter 3
# iOS 8

# Home screen

**Organise your apps**

Your iPhone comes with built-in apps including Phone for calls and Messages for texts. You can get more from the App Store app (see p58). The Home screen is where all your apps live. It's really not just one screen, but several: swipe a finger across from right to left to see the next page. Apps are arranged on a grid four icons across and seven down. You can't leave gaps, except at the bottom right of a page when there are no icons left. But you can change the order of the icons, move them between pages and group them in folders.

The bottom row of icons is fixed, and the same on every page. It can include any four apps.

To rearrange your Home screen, tap and hold any icon until they all start to jiggle. Then tap and hold any icon and drag it

**↓ Every app has an icon. Red badges show when apps have items awaiting your attention.**

around. The others will duck out of the way to let you drop it where you want. Drag it to the side of the screen to move it onto a different page, or to the bottom to add it to the fixed row of icons. Pages are indicated by white dots; dragging an icon to the right of the last page makes another.

If you drag an app icon on top of another, a border appears around the bottom one. Let go to group those two apps in a folder. You can then drop additional apps into the folder (see p46). Notice that your Home screen wallpaper (see p47) has an effect on how folders look, both as icons and when you open them. This might influence your choice of background.

**⬇ Tap and hold an icon and they jiggle. You can then rearrange them and create folders.**

When you've finished rearranging your apps, press the Home button and the icons will stop jiggling again.

To use any app, just tap its icon, and the app's display grows out of the icon to fill the screen. There's no need to close apps; when you want to do something else, just press the Home button to shrink the current app back into your Home screen. Press the Home button twice to see apps you've recently used (see p56).

Sometimes an app's icon is dimmed, with a gradually filling circle. This means the app is still downloading from Apple's servers, either because you've just installed it, it's getting an update (see p60), or your iPhone is busy restoring from a backup (see p34). If you want to prioritise, tap an icon to pause its download, allowing others to complete first; tap it again to resume downloading.

The built-in apps can't be removed. If there are some that you never need, just move them to the last page or hide them in a folder. Any app you've added from the App Store can be deleted. Tap and hold to make the icons jiggle, then tap the cross at the top left of an icon to delete that app. You can get it back free of charge later, but any data that was stored with it, such as game progress, will be lost unless it was kept online, for example by Game Center.

**⬇ Like the Home screen itself, Folders can contain multiple pages – up to 135 apps in total.**

## Using folders

Folders are good for grouping apps by kind. When you make one, iOS names it according to the genre of the first two apps. To change this name, open the folder while the icons are jiggling, then tap the folder name at the top.

Tapping a folder opens it and shows the apps it contains in a three-by-three grid of icons. Each folder can contain up to 15 pages. You could use pages within a folder of games, for example, to hold different genres of game.

Folders increase the chances of forgetting where you've put an app. You can find it using Spotlight (see p48) from the Home screen, or tell Siri, the iPhone's voice-controlled assistant (see p76), to open the app.

# Wallpapers

### Static or dynamic

You can change the wallpapers of the Lock and Home screens to any of Apple's ready-made backgrounds or your own photos.

Open the Settings app and tap Wallpapers in the third group down, and then tap Choose a New Wallpaper. Elements in dynamic wallpapers move at different rates as your iPhone tilts. Still wallpapers slide on a different plane to foreground objects as your iPhone is tilted. That effect can be disabled in Settings > General > Accessibility > Reduce Motion.

Lower down, you can choose from recent photos, images saved from other apps, and any albums you've created. Tap a photo to see how it'll look, and adjust how it fits by pinching and swiping. Finally, tap Set and choose whether to use this as your Lock screen, Home screen or both.

**↓ Your own photos can be added to the backgrounds of the Lock and Home screens.**

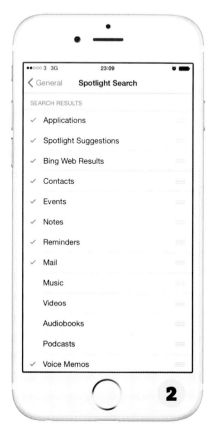

**Spotlight** Spotlight is iOS's search facility. To use it ❶, swipe down with one finger from the middle of the screen on any page of the Home screen (not inside a folder). Spotlight can find apps, contacts, emails and other things stored on your iPhone, as well as stuff from the internet. If it's finding types of items you don't want, open the Settings app and go to General > Spotlight Search ❷. Tap any row to clear the tick next to it and hide those results. You can also change the order in which results will be presented: hold one of the 'grips' (three stacked lines) on the right and drag it up or down.

Some Spotlight results show details such as an event's date or the first few lines of an email. Apps in results display the folder they're stored

in, if any, to their right so that you know where to find them next time.

Spotlight's connection to the internet increases its usefulness: you don't have to explicitly open the iTunes Store, for example, to look for music by an artist ❸, or browse to Wikipedia in Safari to find out more about a subject that's grabbed your attention. Much of the time it'll find what you're looking for as soon as you've typed a few characters.

Enter the name of a major landmark, and Spotlight displays a link to the Maps app so you can get directions to that place. Its online search capabilities even look for breaking and recent news about a location ❹. Whether you're looking for information you've created on your phone or knowledge online, Spotlight should be your first port of call.

# Control Center

**In one place** Control Center provides short-cuts to features. Open it at any time by touching the screen at the bottom and swiping up. This even works on the Lock screen, unless you turn off Settings > Control Center > Access on Lock Screen.

You can quickly set Airplane mode (often required during take-off and landing, but also just a quick way to disable all wireless communications), turn wifi and Bluetooth on or off, enable Do Not Disturb, lock the display orientation and more. Audio play-back controls are here, too, so you can see what's playing, control it, and switch to the app responsible without remembering which it is.

Two Apple wireless features are also here: AirDrop and AirPlay (see p52). AirDrop makes it easy to swap files with owners of other iOS 7 and 8 devices and Macs running OS X 10.10 Yosemite: see support. apple.com/kb/HT5887. Tap AirDrop in Control Center to set whether

**❶ The first three icons control Airplane mode, wifi and Bluetooth. The button faces are white when a feature is on.**

**❷ Tap the moon icon to activate Do Not Disturb (see p39).**

**❸ This control prevents the display from rotating when you turn the iPhone.**

**❹ Screen brightness setting.**

**❺ Any audio that's currently playing is shown here. You can adjust its volume, pause, or skip to the next or previous track. Tap the track name to open the app that's playing it.**

**❻ Tap this icon to use the iPhone's LED flash as a torch.**

**❼ Set a timer in the Clock app.**

**❽ Open the Calculator or Camera app. Sadly, you can't replace these icons with your own choice of apps.**

your device is visible to everyone nearby, only to contacts from your iCloud account, or not at all. When you're visible, the text turns white and confirms your status.

Your iPhone doesn't need to be connected to wifi or a cell network for this: Bluetooth is used to discover other devices and, when you start a transfer, AirDrop creates an encrypted 'peer to peer' wifi connection. Available recipients appear when you tap the Action button in an app to share something ❾.

# AirPlay

### From iPhone to TV or hifi

Your iPhone can stream music and video to devices that support Apple's AirPlay technology, which works over wifi. They include AirPlay-ready speakers, available from many different manufacturers, and Apple's Apple TV, a small black box that connects to your HDTV set. Apple's AirPort Express router also receives AirPlay and can pass on an audio signal to a speaker.

One way to start streaming is to swipe up from the bottom of the screen to reveal Control Centre. The AirPlay icon appears near the bottom right ❶ if any receivers are visible on the wifi network that your iPhone is connected to. Tap the icon and choose a receiver ❷. If you've given your AirPlay device a name, that'll appear here; otherwise it'll just have a generic title. Select an Apple TV and turn on Mirroring, and whatever's on your iPhone screen will appear on the TV

(complete with audio). Or pick an AirPlay speaker, and whatever music is playing will output through that.

Many apps have their own built-in AirPlay features. In Photos, tap to bring up a single photo, then tap the Action button ⬆ and tap the AirPlay icon to put it on TV or Slideshow for a big-screen presentation.

While using almost any app to play a video, you'll see an AirPlay icon. Tap this to show the video on TV (via your Apple TV) while controlling it from your iPhone. (Some apps that show licensed content block AirPlay, so this may not always be possible; but BBC iPlayer supports it, as does YouTube.) Some games, such as Real Racing, use AirPlay to put the action on the TV while showing a completely different display on your iPhone, turning it into a game controller.

### Bluetooth

It's not as smart as AirPlay, and doesn't do video, but Bluetooth is also available to connect a wide range of wireless speakers and headphones. Open the Settings app and tap Bluetooth to see all compatible devices nearby. Check your accessory's instructions to see how to make it 'discoverable'; it should then appear here. Tap its name and follow any instructions to pair it with your iPhone. Having done this once, it should connect automatically whenever it's near.

Bluetooth will drain battery life faster, so turn it off when not in use. You can do this quickly via the Bluetooth icon ❸ in Control Center. It turns white when on.

# Notifications

**What's going on**

Your iPhone can notify you about all kinds of things as they happen, such as emails arriving or calendar events coming up. In the Settings app, tap Notifications to control how this works. Under Include, tap the name of any app to set which method it uses to notify you ❶. Banners pop up at the top of the screen, and you can pull down on many of them to respond without leaving the app you're in. Otherwise, tap to jump straight to the notification's app. If you do neither, the notification fades and can be found later in Notification Center. Alerts pop up in the middle of the display and stick around until dealt with.

Apps normally display a red badge that tells you how many items want your attention, and they can also play sounds. These options can be tailored for each app so that you're only inter-rupted by those you really care about. You can also set whether

each app's notifications appear in the Lock screen; you may want to turn that off for privacy. Some apps have additional options: Messages, for example, lets you choose whether the content of messages is previewed.

To see Notification Centre at any time, swipe down from the very top of the screen ❷. Under Notifications, tap an item to jump to the relevant app, or swipe leftwards across it to find an option to remove that notification from the list, and sometimes additional actions to deal with it.

The Today view ❸ summarises reminders, birthdays and calendar events. You can choose which of these to show by swiping to the bottom (when your iPhone is unlocked) and tapping Edit. You can also turn on widgets here to display information from some apps you've downloaded.

# App Switcher

**Quick change**

If you've already opened several apps, double-click the Home button to reveal the App Switcher. This displays thumbnails of recent contacts and recently used apps, with the current one (or the Home screen) at the far left. Their icons are shown below. Swipe to flip through the apps. When you find the one you want, tap it to switch to it.

Unlike on a Mac or PC, these 'open' apps aren't all using up memory space or battery power, so there's no need to close apps you're not using. If an app seems to have stopped working, swipe its thumbnail upwards and it flies off. You can re-open it if you like.

iOS lets apps 'refresh' in the background so that they're ready when you need them, pre-loaded with current data. The system works out when is a good time to allow this to happen without slowing anything else down, making the best use of available data reception and battery power.

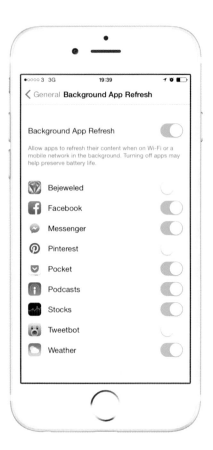

**← Double-tap the Home button and swipe horizontally to see recently used apps.**

**↑ Swipe an app's thumbnail upwards to close it if it sticks, or to kill background tasks.**

**↗ Background App Refresh makes some apps work more effectively, but can be disabled.**

In Settings, you can control this under General > Background App Refresh. If you disable it entirely, apps like Google Maps won't work so well; but you could disable it for apps you don't care about, to minimise battery and data usage. Under Mail, Contacts, Calendars > Show In App Switcher, you can set whether recent contacts, favour-ites or both appear in the top row.

# App Store

**You can do anything**

More than a million apps are available for iOS, of which most run on the iPhone – astonishing when you think it's only been around since 2007, and wasn't even planned to support third-party software. To help you find apps among all these that meet your needs, Apple highlights popular ones and new arrivals on the Featured page you'll see when you open the App Store app.

The Top Charts tab shows the most popular free and paid apps. Tap Categories at the top left of either page to narrow it down to one genre. The Kids category and, under Games, the Educational and Family sub-genres will be useful for parents.

The Explore tab shows apps that are popular based on your location, and popular and curated apps by genre and purpose.

When you can't see what you want straight away, tap Search and enter some keywords.

**⬏ The Featured page shows new apps, with one app on special free offer every week.**

**⬇ Turn on Touch ID for purchases under Settings > Touch ID & Passcode > Use Touch ID For > iTunes & App Store, and you can verify purchases with a fingerprint instead of typing in your iTunes password.**

Swipe through the results, then tap one to read a description of it, see reviews from other customers or find similar apps.

Tap the Action button ⬆ at the top right of an app's page to add it to your Wish List, send it as a gift or share a link. The next icon, depicting three bullet points, displays your Wish List.

To buy an app, tap its price, then tap again after this changes to 'Buy'. Unless you've done so for another purchase in the past 15 minutes, you'll be asked to enter the password for your iTunes account to confirm the purchase.

You can leave the App Store while your app downloads. A dimmed version of its icon appears on the Home screen, with a circle on top that displays a growing segment to indicate progress. Apps larger than 100MB can't be downloaded over a mobile network, only via wifi.

Once you've bought an app, it's yours to install on any device on your iTunes account. You can delete it and re-install it later for free. Tap Updates at the bottom right, then Purchased. Wait for the list to fill, then tap the cloud next to any app to install it.

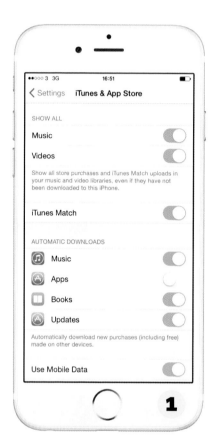

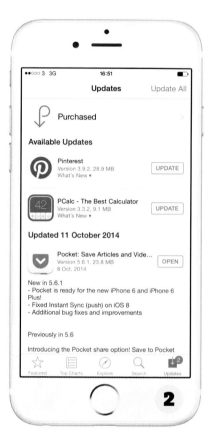

### Updates

Software developers regularly update their apps to fix problems and add new features. Updates are free abd can be installed automatically whenever your device is plugged in and on wifi. Look under Automatic Downloads in the iTunes & App Store page of the Settings app ❶. The relevant item is labelled 'Updates'. If you flick the switch to off, updates can still be installed manually from the Updates tab at the bottom right of the App Store app.

If you allow the App Store to display Notifications (see p54), you'll be told whenever an automatic update has occurred. This information also appears a little way down the App Store's Updates tab ❷, where you can read about the changes made in pending and previous updates.

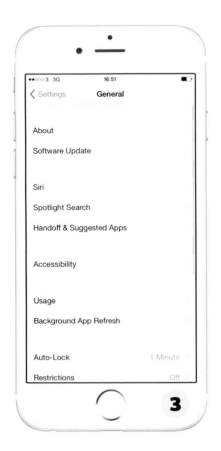

The other Automatic Downloads settings allow new apps and other media purchased from iTunes on your Mac or a PC, or on another iOS device, to be sent to your iPhone as soon as you buy them.

When an update to iOS itself is available ❸, a pop-up alert should inform you. It can be installed immediately, even over a mobile network, provided that your iPhone's battery is over 50% or it's plugged in. If you put off an iOS update, find it later in the Settings app, which displays a number next to General as a reminder. Tap General > Software Update to read about its contents ❹. Before updating iOS, it's a good idea to check that essentials – such as your banking app – are ready for the new version. There could be glitches for the first few days or weeks.

# Settings

**Have it your way**

The Settings app lets you customise the behaviour and appearance of all your iPhone's features, which it groups by function. The first group ❶ deals with network connections, and then there are user interface options ❷ and the huge General subgroup ❸. Further down, you can manage the built-in apps that come with your iPhone and connect to social networks to share things with other users online.

Many headings show an arrowhead ❹ at the right, indicating that they lead to pages of options. Ultimately, each choice is often a simple on or off: notice that the switches are plain white when off, half green when on ❺.

As we guide you through your iPhone's features, we'll refer back to items in Settings and point out where to find them.

**↓ Exploring the Settings app amounts to a tour of the features of your iPhone.**

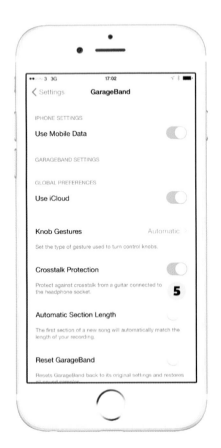

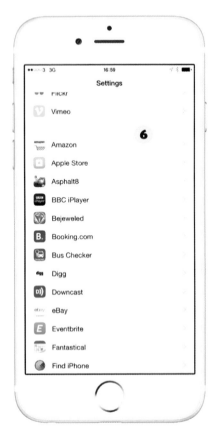

Apps that you've added from the App Store are listed in a group at the bottom of the Settings app ❻, below the one for social networks. The idea is that persistent choices about an app's behaviour are placed here – although some apps add nothing more than a way to check the installed version number, which appears elsewhere in Settings anyway.

Look out for further options within the apps themselves. For example, the iBooks app includes a fly-out panel that lets you tweak its presentation at any time without interrupting your reading (see p112). Many apps tuck their settings away less prominently. Check for a cogwheel icon, which is often the one to tap to reveal advanced features and choices.

# Usage

**Space raiders**    Your iPhone comes with a fixed amount of storage, such as 64GB. A little of this is taken up by iOS, leaving a certain number of gigabytes for storing apps, media, documents and – often a significant element – the photos and videos you've shot.

You can't plug in extra memory, so when your iPhone warns you there's no room to take more pictures or install more apps, you'll need to delete something. But what? In the Settings app, General > About shows you the total amount of storage and how much is in use, but there's another place you can go to see exactly what's taking up space and quickly remove some of it.

Go to Settings > General > Usage and, under the Storage heading, tap Manage Storage. Give your iPhone a moment to

**↓ Games and magazine apps are among those that typically demand the most storage.**

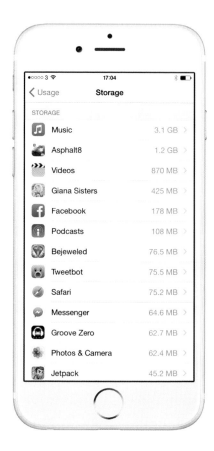

gather data and you'll then see a list of installed apps, starting with those that take up the most space.

Tap an app to confirm the size of it and its data. If you want to delete the app, you can do so from here, but data is trickier; most apps lump all their content under a single 'Documents & Data' item, and few allow it to be deleted from here. If it's possible, the word Edit appears at the top right; tap to pick what to erase. Usually, it's better to open the app and delete files from there if they're taking up too much room.

**↓ Here you can see which videos are stored on your iPhone and hogging space.**

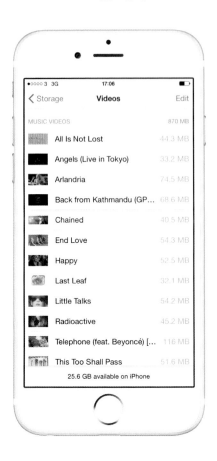

If you delete apps, music or videos bought from iTunes, you'll be able to re-download them later at no cost from the Purchased section in the relevant app. But if any are really important to you, check in the Store first: vendors sometimes discontinue products, and there's then no way to download them again.

Unwanted apps can also be deleted from the Home screen. Hold a finger on an icon, and when they all start to jiggle, tap the cross at the top left. This also removes any data belonging to it. Unless the app stores its data in iCloud or a third-party cloud service, iOS doesn't make it easy to keep a copy of it for later. You can use apps such as PhoneView (for Mac, from ecamm.com) or TouchCopy (for Windows, from wideanglesoftware.com) to get at the data and make a copy.

# Accessibility

***Breaking barriers***

iOS has a range of features to help users with sight, hearing, mobility or other difficulties – and many are more broadly useful than that might suggest. Look under General > Accessibility in the Settings app. For a start, some owners of older iOS devices have complained about the switch to thinner fonts in iOS 7 and 8. It can be alleviated by enabling Bold Text here; you'll need to restart your iPhone for this to take effect.

VoiceOver reads out a description of what's on screen, useful if you can't see it. Invert Colors can help if the glare from white backgrounds in iOS 8 disturbs you (and reducing the screen brightness doesn't help).

The Larger Text setting only affects apps that have been engineered to use iOS's typography engine, Dynamic Type. Apps that support it will reflect the legible font size you've set here.

Reduce Motion eliminates the parallax effect on the Home screen, so that icons and the background don't move independently as your iPhone tilts. This eases one concern for sufferers of vestibular disorders, and it also disables many zoom and pan transitions which can provoke nausea, such as those normally shown when opening and switching apps.

Hearing aid manufacturers have developed devices that work with the iPhone: find out more about them at support.apple.com/kb/HT4526. LED Flash for Alerts will be useful to those who don't hear alert sounds, but can also be handy for anyone who has to maintain silence at work.

Many more accessibility features are available. It's well worth playing around with the settings, but if you depend on such options, and perhaps additional products, to get the best out of your iPhone, a good starting point to find out more is apple.com/accessibility/ios.

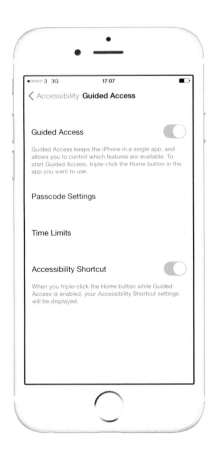

**↑ Guided Access lets you draw around parts of an app's screen that you don't want a user to be able to interact with. They'll still appear, but won't respond.**

## Guided Access

Guided Access is a customisable way to prevent another user interacting with certain regions of the screen. One use for this is so that users with impaired motor skills don't find themselves frustratingly tapping the wrong items. It's also a great way to allow younger children to play with selected apps without being able to run amok on your iPhone, and to limit how long they can play.

When you turn it on (under Settings > General > Accessibility > Guided Access), you can set a passcode that will be required to turn it off again, or use Touch ID. Otherwise, the user can exit this mode and switch to other apps by triple-clicking the Home button.

With Guided Access on, open the app to be used, then triple-click the Home button to set up Guided Access. Use your finger to mark out regions of the screen to disable. Drag the corner points to refine. It works best with apps that operate within one screen. Tap Options if you want to disable access to hardware buttons, motion sensors, and even the touchscreen as a whole, for example to leave a child watching a video.

Tap Start when you're ready to leave the user to it. Triple-click the Home button to stop or change settings; to drop back in, tap Resume.

# Restrictions

**Better safe than sorry** Even with a passcode or Touch ID active, there's a risk you might leave your iPhone unattended and unlocked. Perhaps you're watching a video, and put it down without pausing; the iPhone won't go to sleep and lock itself. If someone else does find it unlocked, they're still barred from a lot of actions, such as disabling Find My iPhone or removing your iCloud account, by the requirement to enter your Apple ID password (something that may gradually be replaced by Touch ID). But other damage can be caused. Changes might not even be malicious: it's easy for a small child to delete apps, which you can always get back, along with the data contained in them, which in some cases you can't.

If you're deliberately leaving your iPhone in someone else's care, and especially if that person is young and/or foolish, you should definitely consider setting some limits. Open the Settings app, tap General in the third group down, then tap Restrictions in the fifth group. All the items but the first here will be faded out to begin with. Tap Enable Restrictions and choose a four-digit passcode – ideally different to the one that unlocks your device, in case that becomes compromised. (Note that the Simple Passcode setting has no bearing on this; it's always four digits.)

So far, nothing has changed about the way your iPhone behaves. But you can now put a secondary level of protection in place against physical access. The options let you deny access to apps, features, the ability to change important settings, and so on.

The top group controls access to Safari and some hardware features. The second group controls access to Apple's Stores, and restricts the ability to install and remove apps and to make in-app purchases.

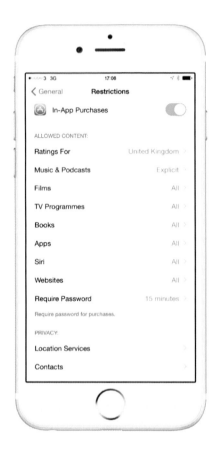

**← If you only set up one restriction, change Require Password to Immediately to close the window of risk for accidental purchases. Higher up, you can also turn off In-App Purchases.**

The third group of options censors content from the Stores. Require Password is a vital setting if a child has access to your device: with the default of 15 minutes, if you were to enter your Apple ID password to buy something, then hand your phone over, they could buy *any* apps or in-app purchases up to your credit card limit for the next 15 minutes. Change the setting to Immediately and you'll avoid this scenario – and be sure not to tell the child your password 'just for this one thing'.

The next two groups protect your privacy by preserving your existing choices made elsewhere in Settings, such as which apps can access your private data, and restrict changes to accounts and other important features. The final group contains two options for Game Center. When turned off, the amount of contact your child has with strangers when playing games is restricted. As with all parental controls, this is not a substitute for supervision.

To change the options later, or to carry out any of the operations you've restricted, you'll need to come back to this page, tap Disable Restrictions, and enter your Restrictions passcode. After making changes, tap Enable Restrictions and set the code again. Take care not to forget it.

# Health

**Vital statistics**

There are thousands of apps to help you monitor your health and fitness. Some of them use the iPhone's sensors to estimate how many steps you've taken, how many flights of stairs you've climbed, and even how far you've walked or cycled, using the iPhone's GPS capability. Others pair with accessories, from fitness bands to scales, that analyse your body composition. iOS 8's Health app consolidates these readings on a single dashboard for you to review, although apps need to explicitly be written to work with it.

You needn't buy accessories to make use of Health, though, because it also allows for manual entry of data, from calories to inhaler usage through to vitamin and mineral intake.

Tap Health Data to browse these, and tap an item to add data or review readings on a chart. Your most important items can be added to Health's Dashboard. Tap Sources

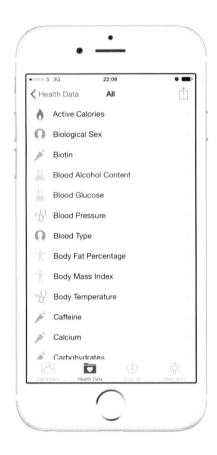

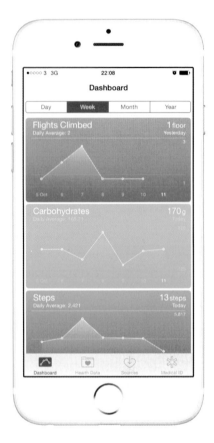

**↑ Health can monitor 68 attributes of your body and exercise to help monitor your progress.**

**↗ You choose which metrics appear on Health's dashboard for regular monitoring.**

**← External devices, including the Apple Watch, can feed data into Health, and read from it.**

to see which of your apps work with Health and to choose which metrics each can read and write.

Tap Medical ID to manage details of your medical conditions, medications and emergency contacts. If someone finds you unresponsive, they'll be able to access this at the Lock screen when, having swiped, they see options for Emergency, then Medical ID.

# Safari

**Slicker surfing**

Safari is like any other web browser at first glance: you type an address into the box at the top and the page loads below. You may be a little disconcerted when you start reading the page and all the toolbars disappear. This is to give you room to read; to get them back, scroll up a bit, or tap once at the top or bottom. Remember you can tap the very top of the screen in most iOS apps to scroll back to the top of a long page.

When you have several pages open, the Tab view stacks them up. Turn your iPhone sideways (as below) and the tabs spread out into a grid.

Tap the URL bar to show favourite and frequently visited sites. Pull downwards on that view to add the current site to your favourites. To bookmark a page, tap the Action button ⬆ and pick Add Bookmark. Or choose Add to Reading List to save the page for offline viewing.

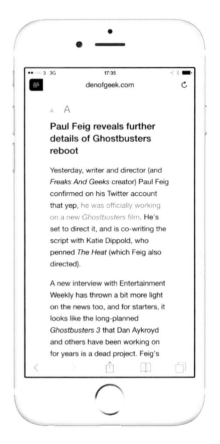

↑ **Tap the Action button** ⬆ **to reveal this Action sheet, which appears throughout iOS. Among other things, a page can be shared on social networks.**

← **Tap the overlapping squares to open a new tab (+), turn on Private mode (which avoids storing details of visited pages) for this tab, or switch tabs.**

↑ **On pages that contain a large amount of continuous text, tap the icon that appears to the left of the site's address to open Reader, which strips the page down to just the main text and images. The two letter 'A's at the top left of this view can be used to adjust the text size. Tap the same icon to return to the normal page view.**

# Mail

**Get the message**

If you logged in to iCloud when setting up your iPhone, the Mail app will already have the details of your mac .com, me.com or icloud.com email account. In Settings, under iCloud, turn Mail on or off to dictate whether mail for this account is received on your iPhone. Your iCloud mailboxes and emails are all synced between all your Apple devices automatically.

To add other accounts to Mail, such as a Gmail account, go to Settings > Mail, Contacts, Calendars. Tap Add Account and enter the details.

Open the Mail app and you'll see your accounts listed in the Mailboxes page. If you have more than one active email account, they're listed here below an 'All Inboxes' folder: tap this to show all incoming messages on all your accounts. Tap an account name at the top to see just its Inbox, or under Accounts to see all its folders.

← **Messages are grouped into conversations if the Organise by Thread setting is on. Tap an item to see the whole thing. A blue dot denotes an unread message, while orange means one you've flagged up. Swipe leftwards just a little on an item for actions. Use Mail's Swipe Options setting to choose what longer swipes left and right do.**

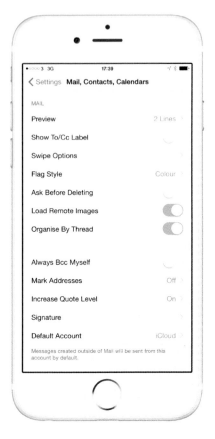

← **To refer to other messages while writing one, drag downwards from top of the draft to store it at the bottom of the screen. Tap there to get it back.**

→ **Don't look for options in the Mail app itself: they're mostly found in the Settings app under 'Mail, Contacts, Calendars'.**

# Siri

**Your inflectible friend**

Siri lets you control the iPhone with your voice. Hold down the Home button until you hear a tone, then speak. If you're on mains power, you can also just say 'Hey Siri'. Now ask a question ('Where can I eat pizza?'), give an instruction ('Play Michael Bublé'), or dictate messages. As long as you have internet access, Siri will respond. Tap the question mark at the bottom left to see examples.

Customise Siri in Settings > General > Siri. He or she responds through the iPhone's loudspeaker unless Voice Feedback is set to Hands-free Only. Tap My Info and choose your record from Contacts so that Siri can interpret requests such as 'Show me the way home'. The Language setting not only governs Siri's accent, but guides its expectations of your diction.

**↑ Siri can send emails, text messages, Facebook updates and tweets for you, and this works even when your iPhone is locked, unless you disable General > Touch ID & Passcode > Siri. (Doing so also prevents you making calls or choosing music by holding the centre button on your EarPod clicker while the iPhone is locked.)**

↑ **Your tummy is rumbling and you want something to eat in a hurry. This is no time to be typing into search engines! Just tell Siri what you want to eat and it'll come up with suitable restaurants nearby. Tap one to see its location and phone number, then tap the preview map to have the Maps app guide you straight there.**

↑ **Siri is capable of having a proper exchange with you to make sure it has all the details it needs to send an email or a text message to the right person. It's also able to take notes and set up alarms, reminders and events. It's even sensible enough to warn you if an event clashes with something already on your schedule.**

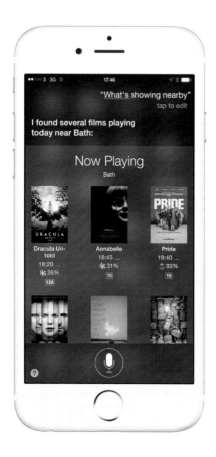

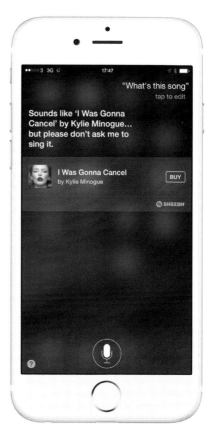

↑ Ask Siri what's showing at the cinema and it'll pull up listings for the nearest places. Siri always repeats your words on screen as text so you can see what it thought you said; if it misheard, you can tap its interpretation of your words, rather than repeating yourself, and correct them using the keyboard to rerun the query.

↑ When you hear a great song, you longer need to use an app like Shazam to find out what it is. Just ask Siri. It will listen for a short time and then come back to you with an answer. You can buy the song straight away. If you don't, it gets added to a special tab in your iTunes Store Wish List for songs tagged with Siri.

# Keyboard

**Don't be typecast** iOS 8 has a built-in virtual keyboard that appears when- ever you need to enter text. But you can also install alternative keyboards from the App Store. Look under Explore > Utilities > Featured Utilities. After installing a keyboard app, open it for details on its use and how to turn it on. You'll be directed to Settings > General > Keyboard > Keyboards. The list here shows enabled key- boards. Tap Add New Keyboard… to turn on others that you've installed. Third-party keyboards are grouped near the top.

Tap anywhere you can type to reveal the regular keyboard, then tap the globe/Emoji key (bottom left) and choose a listed keyboard. Delete a keyboard's app to uninstall it. Only Apple's key- board is used when you're asked for your Apple ID password.

**↓ Apple's keyboard suggests words you may type next, and it learns from previous typing.**

# Maps

**Find your way**
You can install Google Maps from the App Store if you prefer, but Apple's Maps app, pre-installed on your iPhone, is actually very good, and also works as a free satnav. Open Maps and you'll see the map screen overlaid by toolbars. Tap once to hide or show them. Spread two fingers apart to zoom in, and swipe to move around. Type the name or address of where you're looking for, and tap and hold on the map to drop a pin at a precise location **1**. Tapping a pin then shows the address, and you can request directions to it.

Tap the arrowhead at the bottom left to show where you are now, and again to show which way you're facing. Tap the 'i' to view the map in 3D; this only works properly in some major locations **2**. An option to take a 3D Flyover Tour may appear too.

The 'i' also enables you to switch to Satellite view, which adds photographic textures, and

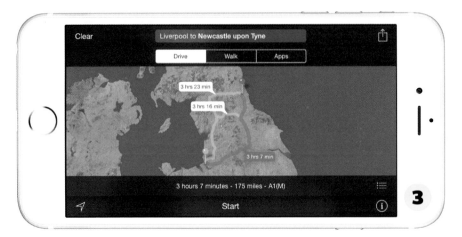

traffic density can be turned on here to spot delays. You can also report problems with map data to Apple.

After searching for or pinning a location, tap the Action button ⬆ to add it to a contact, or tap the same icon again to add it to your favourites, accessed from the search bar. Tap the arrow at the top left for driving, walking or (in some locations) public transport directions. Supply a start and end point, then tap Route for an overview ❸, sometimes with alternatives. Tap Start and the app uses the iPhone's GPS to follow you and speak directions. To mute it, tap for the toolbars, then tap the speaker icon.

**Clock**   The Clock app's four functions are accessed from the bottom of its screen **❶**. In Settings > Sounds > Ringer and Alerts, turning off Change with Buttons means the slider sets the ringtone and alarm volume, while the phone's buttons set it for other sounds. Stopwatch times laps, while Timer counts down a duration.

**Compass**   When you open the iPhone's Compass app **❷**, you'll be asked to tilt the phone to calibrate it. It'll stay calibrated for a while. Tap the screen to record your current heading and then turn; a red arc shows the divergence, but the maths is left to you. Swipe from leftwards to reveal an inclinometer.

### Weather

There are lots of pretty weather apps available, but Apple's will brighten up your day with its animations even if the forecast isn't good. The screen changes colour to reflect the time of day and the weather ❸, so you'll see gorgeous snow, rain, even lightning, or slowly moving clouds and blue sky.

Tap the temperature to reveal how warm it actually feels, the chance of rain and more. The hourly forecasts can be swiped across, and indicate the times of sunrise and sunset too. Swipe anywhere else to switch to the next location in the app's list ❹, which can be revealed by 'pinching' the screen (move two fingers inwards). Tap '+' at the bottom right of this screen to add a location. Zoom (move two fingers outwards) to go back.

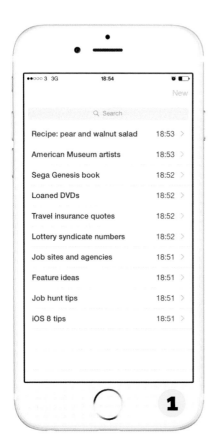

### Notes

The Notes app is an informal, no-frills scrapbook for bits and bobs of text ❶. You could use it for a recipe or a shopping list, or to store information you found on a web page. But remember you also have the Reminders app (see opposite) for to-do lists, and the Calendar app (see p86) for notes about events.

Tap New at the top right to make a new note. Add some text ❷, then tap Done. Notes are synced to iCloud for access on your other Apple devices and via icloud.com on any PC. Each note's name is its first line.

To delete a note from the list, swipe right to left across its name, then tap Delete. You can also delete a note from its own screen, where you'll also find an Action button ⬆ to share it in various ways or print it.

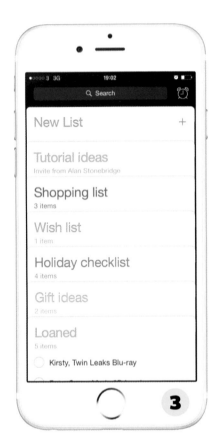

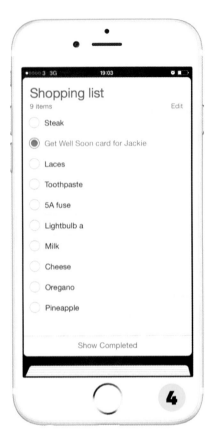

**Reminders**  The Reminders app lets you create simple but effective to-do lists. It integrates with iOS's Notifications system (see p54) to jog your memory at a requested time, and using the iPhone's 'geofencing' capability you can even tell it to give you a nudge when you arrive at or leave a given place.

Lists are shown like cards in a stack. Tap a name ❸ to view one ❹; tap again to go back. Tap the circle next to an item to mark it as completed, or swipe leftwards across it to delete it. Completed items are just hidden; you can refer back to them or correct a mistake by tapping Show Completed. Tap Edit when viewing a list, then tap Sharing to invite other iCloud users with whom you want to collaborate on that list.

# Calendar

**Make a date**

Keep track of your schedule in Apple's Calendar app. It can maintain multiple calendars to which you can assign colours, so that when their events are all shown on the same timeline you can see which are which.

While holding your iPhone in portrait (tall) orientation, create a calendar by tapping Calendars at the bottom of the screen, then Edit, then Add Calendar, under the list of those that already exist.

Zoom out of the current day by tapping at the top left to see the Month view **❶**, which scrolls vertically. Tap there again for a view of the year. If you're looking for a particular event and don't know its date, tap the magnifying glass to show a list of events, which will update as you type into the search box above it. The Week view is accessed by turning the iPhone to landscape.

The iPhone 6 Plus exclusively enables you to switch between special Day, Week, Month and

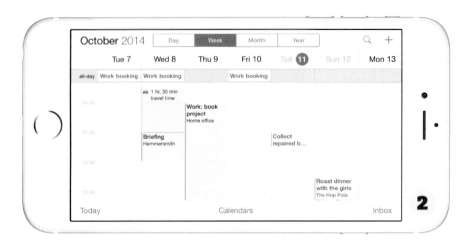

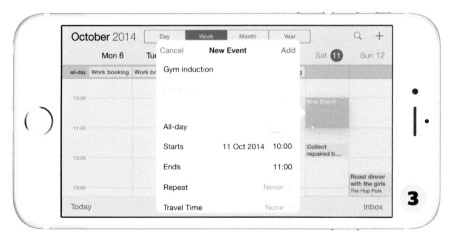

Year views in this orientation ❷. Week view scrolls horizontally and vertically. In the Day and Week views, you can pinch to zoom in or out.

Tap '+' at the top right of any portrait view to create an event, or tap and hold on the Day or Week view, then drag it to a start time. Add details of the event in the form that appears ❸. These can include a location, end time, whether the event repeats and how often, which calendar to add it to, and who to invite via email. The default calendar for events, how far ahead of an event an alert is displayed, and much more can be tailored in Settings > Mail, Contacts, Calendars.

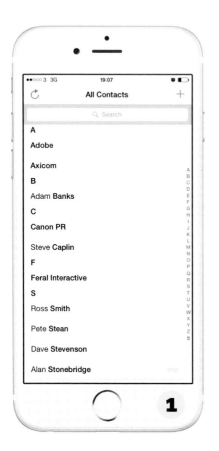

### Contacts

Details of people you know can be managed in two places: in the Contacts app ❶ and in the Contacts tab of the Phone app. Both show you the same list. Tap '+' at the top right to add someone's details ❷, which as well as phone numbers and email addresses can include their postal address, partner, social network handles and any notes you want to add.

A search bar is constantly available at the top . Contacts can be put into groups, which makes it easier to temporarily hide some or quickly send a message to several at once. Tap Groups at the top left of the list. Frustratingly, you can't create groups on your iPhone. You must use the Contacts app on a Mac or go to icloud.com in a desktop web browser.

## Social media

Some of the iPhone's built-in apps, and many others, can post directly to Facebook, Twitter, Flickr and Vimeo, and, when you install apps that provide extensions, to many other networks and services. You can connect to the social networks mentioned above in the seventh group in Settings. You'll also find links here to install those services' apps, but you can post to your accounts from other apps just by signing in. Connecting to Facebook adds your friends and their avatar photos to Contacts, and birthdays appear in Calendar. Photos can be retrieved from Twitter, too.

Tap the Action button ⬆ in an app to get a sheet with icons for social networks **3**. Pick one to post your link, photo or whatever **4**.

# Phone

**Yes, it's a phone too!**

It's a sign of how far mobiles have come that the 'phone' part of iPhone is just another app. It comes up automatically when a call is received. To make a call, tap the Phone icon on the Home screen. When no call is in progress, you'll see icons at the bottom for Favourites, Recents, Contacts, Keypad and Voicemail. Pick Keypad to dial manually.

Favourites are effectively speed dials; tap this tab, then tap '+' at the top to add people you need to call regularly to this handy list. For others, tap Contacts, which takes you to the same place as the Contacts app.

Under Recents, you can view all calls or just those you've missed. Icons next to each call indicate whether it was incoming or outgoing, and whether it was a voice or FaceTime call (see p92).

Nuisance callers can be blocked. Tap the 'i' to the right of any call in Recents, then scroll down and tap Block this Caller. If it's one of your existing contacts, incoming calls from all their numbers will be blocked, along with FaceTime calls from associated email addresses. The list of blocked callers can be amended in the Settings app: Phone > Blocked.

The Voicemail tab is designed to give you access to Visual Voicemail. This hooks in to your mobile network's voicemail system and presents a list of recent voicemails on screen. Tap one to play it; you can also delete it here, or ring the caller back. If your tariff doesn't support Visual Voicemail, this tab will simply call voicemail for you in the normal way.

During a call, when the iPhone is held up to your ear, the screen goes blank and won't respond to accidental touches. Take it away from your ear and an options screen appears. From this, you can mute the iPhone's microphone so that the caller can't hear you; show the keypad to dial

numbers; switch the call to the iPhone's speaker; add another caller for conference calls (subject to network); switch to a FaceTime video call (see p92); or open Contacts to look something up. You can also press the Home button and go to another app. A green bar will appear at the top of the screen to remind you the call is still ongoing; tap it to go back to the Phone app.

↖ **When your iPhone rings, you can pick up the call, decline it (sending the caller to your network's voicemail), set a reminder to call the person back, or send them a preset message.**

↑ **During a call, tap Keypad if you need to press keys. You can also switch to other apps without cutting off the call.**

# FaceTime

**I see you calling**

FaceTime is Apple's alternative to Skype and other video and voice over IP (VoIP) telephony services. When it was first introduced, it would only let you make video calls over wifi (ultimately, via landline broadband rather than a cell network), but you can now use it over a mobile connection too. However, if you're on a tariff with a limited data allowance, you'll probably still want to use a wifi connection if at all possible to avoid using up your quota and incurring extra charges. Picture quality depends on the speed of your connection, but Apple's technology makes a good job of getting the most from it.

FaceTime calls can be started in two ways. In someone's contact sheet in the Contacts or Phone app, tap the video camera or phone receiver icon next to the word FaceTime. These appear for every contact for whom you have either a phone number or an email address, under the assumption that one of them might be associated with a FaceTime-compatible device: that is, an iPhone, iPad, iPod touch or recent Mac.

You can also start a call in the standalone FaceTime app. When you open the app, don't be freaked out by the ghostly figure in the background: it's you, live on your iPhone's front camera. Video calls use the front-facing camera by default to make you visible to the caller, but you can tap a control during the call to switch to the main camera at the rear, perhaps to show the caller something or let other people in the room say hello without all crowding behind you. The iPhone can be turned to either orientation, even mid-call, as you prefer.

Your full contacts list is available in the app, and the above method works again. But when you add a contact to Favorites, you're asked which

← **FaceTime works between any two iOS devices, so you can call someone from your iPhone and they might reply on their iPad. You can set any number of your own iOS devices to respond to the same FaceTime contact, such as your email address.**

→ **FaceTime is also supported on the Mac, so you can hold conversations between mobile and desktop users. The iPhone's advantage is that you can get in touch from almost anywhere.**

of their contact methods to use. A FaceTime caller ID can be either a mobile number or an Apple ID (an email address registered with Apple), so you may have to ask which of someone's details to use. You can then tell the app whether to add the ID to Favorites for FaceTime (video) or FaceTime Audio. Voice-only calls allow you to use FaceTime both to avoid call charges (though data charges will still apply if you're on a metered mobile tariff) and to get higher-quality audio.

When your iPhone alerts you that someone is trying to reach you via FaceTime, you can respond in the same ways as to a regular phone call. Buttons on the caller ID screen let you answer, set a reminder to yourself to call back, or reply with a preset text message if you're busy. Under FaceTime in the Settings app, you can disable FaceTime altogether or customise it. Choose which of the email addresses associated with your Apple ID can be used by someone else to start a FaceTime call with you (or none at all). Your iPhone's phone number is always on this list too.

Under Caller ID, you can choose which of your contact details is shown when you make a FaceTime call. Try to make sure it's set to something that your friends will recognise as you when you call.

At the bottom of FaceTime's settings is a link to a Blocked list, which, as with phone calls and messages, you can use to stop nuisance communications. Tap Add New and choose someone from your Contacts list to block. This adds all of their contact methods. Individual methods can be removed, but if they use their mobile number as their caller ID for FaceTime, call blocking makes no distinction between the two – you can only block both or neither. Block unknown callers by tapping 'i' next to their call in the list of recent calls.

The Video and Audio tabs in the FaceTime app naturally reflect only FaceTime calls.

**→ Although video chat is the obvious purpose of FaceTime, you can also use it for audio-only calls. Compared to normal voice calls, they offer higher quality and, if you use wifi or have data allowance on your tariff, won't cost you a penny.**

# Voice Memos

**Your audio notepad**

The Voice Memos app lets you record your thoughts, or anything going on around you, such as a lecture. Tap the big red button to start a memo. Recording will continue even if you switch to another app or lock the iPhone; the top bar turns red, and tapping it returns you to Voice Memos.

Tap the red button again to pause. Tap Done when you're finished and give the recording a name. Tap your new memo in the list ❶, then tap the Action button ⬆ to share it via AirDrop, text or email. Note that memos longer than 15 minutes won't send.

Or tap the blue Edit option and then the blue square icon to show the start and end points of your recording as red bars ❷. Drag these to trim the memo. Press Play ❸ to check what's between the markers. (Tap the speaker icon ❹ to switch output to the earpiece for privacy.) Tap Trim ❺ to save your changes.

# Messages

### SMS or iMessage?

To send a text (SMS) or picture message (MMS), open the Messages app and tap the pencil icon at the top right. Type the name or number of the recipient, or tap '+' to pick one from Contacts. Names shown in black haven't been messaged before from your iPhone. Those in green have sent or received texts. Those in blue are available to communicate with via iMessage, Apple's own service which works only for users of an iPhone, iPad, iPod touch or Mac.

iMessages are handled by the same app. They're sent over the internet, so they're free via wifi but count towards your data allowance on cellular (though very little, unless you send pictures). They're not charged as texts by your network. The Messages app will always use iMessage if the recipient is compatible and if you've activated it in the Settings app: tap Messages, then iMessage ❶ (you may need to sign in).

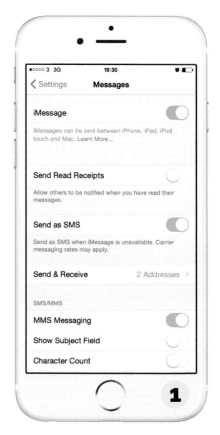

iMessages appear in blue bubbles. If iMessage can't be used, the app will send your message as SMS or MMS, depending on its content. These appear in green bubbles. You can disable SMS/MMS and rely on iMessage, but then you can't text with users of non-Apple mobile phones.

Tap a conversation on Messages' main screen to view it ❷; type a new message in the box at the bottom. To see the times of messages, swipe right to left. To delete one or more messages, double-tap one and pick More. Tap Details to suppress notifications for a conversation, and to give a name to an iMessage group conversation by pulling downwards.

The Phone app (see p90) lets you respond to calls with preset text messages. Define these in Settings > Phone > Respond with Text.

# Passbook

**Papers, please**

The Passbook app is a place to keep digital loyalty cards, cinema tickets, boarding passes, coupons and more ❶. These items can be added by various methods. When you book tickets, a company might email them to you in a Passbook-ready format. Tap the attachment. When you arrive at the venue, just open Passbook, and it'll know where you are and display the ticket you need.

Passes can also be added by scanning special barcodes with the app or by downloading them from websites. Some apps generate passes – the Starbucks and Apple Store apps, for example. Tap Apps for Passbook at the bottom of the Passbook app to see relevant apps where you are ❷. Take-up is still limited so far.

Note that iOS offers suggestions based on your location if the bottom two switches in Settings > General > Handoff & Suggested Apps are turned

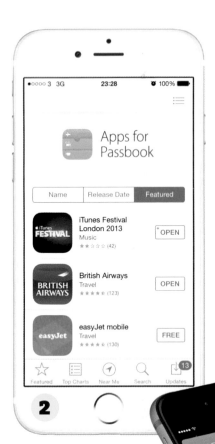

on. Even if you don't have a business's app installed, its icon may appear at the bottom left of the Lock screen and leftmost in the App Switcher (see p56) as a shortcut to download it.

**Apple Pay**

The iPhone 6 is the first Apple device to include an NFC (near-field communication) chip. This is to support Apple Pay, a new service that brings your wallet into your phone. You scan your existing credit or debit cards into Passbook, then just touch your iPhone to any contactless till point to pay from your card. It'll also work on websites.

Apple needs to get the necessary banking agreements in place in each country to make this work beyond the US, and stores may or may not support it, but it seems a very promising system because of its simplicity for the user: you don't need to open a new account with anyone or remember any passwords. A touch of your fingerprint confirms the transaction.

# Camera

**Quick shot** Your iPhone has two cameras, each for photos and video. The front-facing FaceTime camera, above the screen, is handy for video chat and the occasional self-portrait. The rear iSight camera offers better quality and resolution for photography and filming. You can access them both by opening the Camera app; swap between them by tapping the camera icon.

The camera's various modes are shown in a strip next to the live preview: regular 4:3 photos, square photos, panoramas, videos and time lapses. Swipe across the screen to switch mode. Spreading two fingers apart on the screen applies digital zoom to stills or video. This enlarges the area you want, but reduces sharpness; you're just magnifying pixels.

The lightning bolt icon controls whether the LED flash is always on, off, or will fire if needed. HDR ❶ stands for 'high dynamic range': this blends multiple exposures into an image with more detail in high-lights and shadows. Sometimes the tone might look unnatural, so to hedge your bets you can turn on Keep Normal Photo in the Settings app, under Photos & Camera, to store a non-HDR version at the same time. This uses more storage. In the same place, you can turn on a grid in the Camera app to help you compose shots according to the Rule of Thirds, and set the Video mode to record at 60 frames per second instead of 30.

Tap the trio of circles to choose a filter to apply to photos ❷. There are eight: Noir, Chrome, Instant, Tonal, Transfer, Mono, Fade and Process. The circles become coloured when an effect is applied (even if it's Mono). Filters are previewed on the iPhone as you compose shots. These effects aren't irreversible: they can be turned off or changed in the Photos app (see p102). Filters can be applied to panoramas only after they're taken.

Tap any spot to focus on it and set the exposure there, or tap and hold to lock the focus, then slide up or down to adjust the exposure ❸. Tap the clock icon ❹ to set a three or 10-second timer that counts down when the round 'shutter release' button (or a volume button) is pressed, after which the iPhone takes a rapid series of photos. To take a burst without a timer, hold down the shutter release. When recording video, a second button is shown to take a still photo (at video resolution) without stopping. To shoot a panorama, select that mode, hold the camera upright and, as instructed on screen, turn to capture the scene around you.

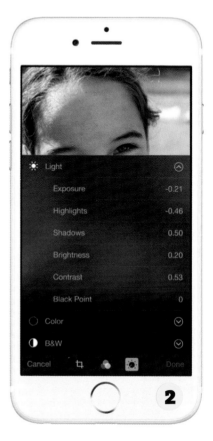

### Photos

The Photos app makes it easier to manage the large numbers of snaps you're likely to take with your iPhone. In this it's helped by the fact that when you shoot, the iPhone captures your location, date and time, providing criteria for sorting.

Open the app and you can zoom right out to see tiny thumbnails of all your pics by year. Tap one to zoom in to Collections, where photos are shown in chronological order grouped by broad location, such as city. Tap again to break these down into Moments **1**, which reflect more specific locations, and once more to fill the screen with one photo.

When looking at years or Collections, hold your finger on a thumbnail to quickly magnify the view. Slide around the screen until you find a photo that interests you, then lift your finger to zoom in all the way. When viewing a single photo, tap Edit at the top right for editing tools: colour adjustments ❷, rotate, preset filters ❸ (see p100) and crop ❹ (which automatically tries to straighten a misaligned horizon). All are 'non-destructive', so you can go back and re-edit later. You can also access these tools directly from the Camera app.

To organise photos, tap Albums. Tap the magnifying glass to find photos by location. Under Shared, you can create online albums. Share photos in other ways wherever you see 'Share' or the Action button ⬆️.

# Chapter 4
# iTunes and iCloud

# Music

**Your sounds everywhere**

When Apple introduced the iPod, it depended on a connection to a Mac to get music. Today, your iPhone can access Apple's iTunes Store directly over wifi or your cell network, so there's no need to sync with a computer (although you still can: see p116).

Open the Settings app and go to iTunes & App Store, signing in to your iTunes account with your Apple ID username and password if you haven't already. If you enable Show All Music here, every track you've ever bought from the iTunes Store will be listed on your iPhone. But it's not actually stored on the iPhone until you decide to download or play it.

Open the Music app and tap the cloud icon next to a track or album ❶ to download it and keep it on your iPhone. Or tap the track name to play it from the cloud: it'll just stay on your iPhone temporarily.

If you have music not bought from iTunes, you can pay a small fee to subscribe to iTunes Match (apple.com/itunes/itunes-match) and upload it from your Mac or PC to the cloud so that you can access it as above.

At the bottom of the Music app's screen are different ways to view your tracks. You can tap More and drag other category icons to here. Or turn your iPhone sideways to browse album artwork in a grid ❷.

Tap Now Playing to see what you're hearing, pause it or skip to the next or previous track. You can also do this in Control Center (see p50).

The Genius tab presents mixes of your tracks that iTunes thinks will work well together. On the Now Playing page ❸, tap Create to use the current track as the seed for an automatically generated Genius Playlist.

# Videos

**Watch via wifi** Videos can be synced (copied) to your iPhone from the iTunes app on a Mac or a PC, but as with music, you can also buy films and TV episodes directly from the iTunes Store (see p110).

Either way, your content can then be viewed in the Videos app.

Open the app and you'll find all your past purchases of movies, TV shows and music videos. At the top left of each video category is a link to the same category on the iTunes Store. A cloud icon beside a music video indicates that it's in the cloud. A tiny cloud in the corner of a film or TV thumbnail means the same thing; tap the item to show its details, with a cloud icon at the top right.

Tap the cloud icon to download the item to your iPhone, and you can then view it. This is only permitted if you're connected to wifi, rather than your cell network, since video files are very large. Public wifi hotspots may baulk, too. So if you're planning to watch

**↑ Tap the screen while a video is playing to see the playback controls. Drag the play head along to move to any point.**

**← Videos stored on your iPhone can be played at any time. To download purchases from the cloud, you'll need to be on a wifi connection.**

while away from home, download the videos you want in advance. (Other Apple devices tethered to your iPhone's Personal Hotspot – see p36 – won't be prevented from downloading videos, but be wary of running up extra data charges if you do so.)

Tap the artwork for a movie or TV show to see a summary of it. The Related tab offers suggestions for similar items. Long videos typically come with a chapter list, and the Videos app will also remember your playback position, as long as you leave this option enabled under Videos in the Settings app.

While you're watching a video, the playback controls hide themselves; just tap once to bring them back. You can drag the playback head from side to side to go forward or back, moving it up or down the screen to adjust the rate of 'scrubbing' from high-speed all the way down to fine.

The Shared tab at the bottom of the app's main screen lets your iPhone play content from any iTunes libraries you've made available from the iTunes app on a Mac or PC over your wifi network via Home Sharing.

# iTunes Store

**Media on tap**
The iTunes icon on your iPhone takes you to Apple's online store for music, films, TV shows, audiobooks and ringtones. Open the app and you can browse the iTunes Store by category from the icons at the bottom of the screen. Tap Genres at the top left to help you find what you're looking for. Audiobooks and ringtones appear when you tap the More button.

Within each category you can see current Featured items or Charts of the most popular under various headings. If flicking through these doesn't satisfy your needs, tap Search and try a title or artist name. Tap More at the top right of the results to restrict what media are shown.

Tap a track name in the Store to listen to a sample. Look for thumbnails marked with a Play symbol to watch film trailers and samples of TV episodes. To buy an item, tap its price tag, then tap the Buy badge that replaces it and enter your Apple ID password to confirm. The first time you buy from a new iPhone, you'll be asked for your card's security code.

To buy with an iTunes gift card instead, scroll to the bottom of any category page and tap Redeem. If your gift card has a box around its code you can just point your iPhone's camera at it; or enter the code manually.

Any item that's over 100MB will require a wifi connection to download, although you can buy it over a cell connection and download it later. To find previous purchases, tap More, then Purchased. The Genius option alongside that shows other items Apple recommends for your tastes.

While you're downloading a purchase, you can still do other things both in the iTunes Store app and in any other app. But if the download is hogging your bandwidth and you need to do something else online, you can pause downloads by tapping More, then Downloads, and tapping

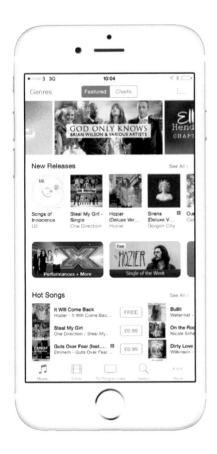

any item in the list. The More icon shows a red badge indicating how many downloads are in progress.

When viewing an item, you can tap the Action button ⬆ at the top right to share a link to it, send it as a gift or add it to your Wish List. View your Wish List by tapping the icon that shows three bullet points. Also here is a history listing of the Previews you've recently viewed.

**⬉ The latest releases are promoted under Featured in each category. You can refine what's shown by genre, by searching, or by looking at personalised Genius recommendations.**

**⬆ You can continue browsing the store while song previews play. A bar at the top lets you stop or buy what's playing.**

# iBooks

**Reading matter**

iBooks is Apple's brand name for electronic books. They appear in iTunes Store searches, but you can switch to the free iBooks app and tap Featured, Top Charts or Search to browse all that's available. As in the iTunes Store app, you can tap Categories at the top left to narrow the range of what's presented when browsing the iBookstore. Some items in this store are free iBooks, including out-of-copyright classics.

Tap My Books to view what you have downloaded in a grid. Books that haven't been downloaded to your iPhone show a cloud icon. Tap a book's cover to download it. Pull down on the shelves to reveal a search bar.

If you prefer, tap the bullet point icon at the top left to switch to a list view, which provides options to sort your books based on title, author, category, and how recently you read them – handy if you have several on the go.

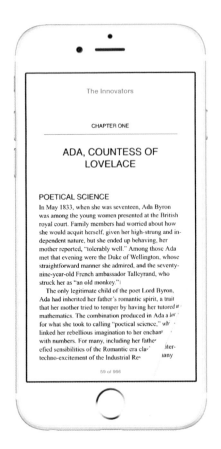

← **Tap the cloud icon to download a purchased book. Tap any book cover to open and read it.**

↑ **Flip the pages by swiping a finger from right to left.**

↗ **The controls at the top right let you set font, size and contrast (not for PDFs). Tap the page to see or hide the icons.**

To organise books in collections, tap Select at the top right, tap some books, then tap Move to choose or create a collection. Swipe horizontally or tap the current collection's name (top centre) to switch between them.

You can also store PDF files in iBooks. Tap and hold on a PDF, for example in an email attachment, and pick Open in iBooks.

# Newsstand

## *Magazines on the move*

Despite its small size, the iPhone's Retina HD display is practical for reading magazines and newspapers too. Open the Newsstand app and tap Store to browse the thousands available. Top titles and hot topics are shown on the front page. Tap Categories at the top left to browse a particular subject.

What distinguishes Newsstand publications from other apps is that new editions appear daily, weekly or monthly, which you can buy individually or on subscription. Apps listed as 'free' are usually empty until you buy one or more issues. Once the app has downloaded, tap its cover in Newsstand to purchase issues.

The Action button ⬆ lets you share a link to a Newsstand publication, but you can't add it to your wish list or give it as a gift.

↓ **Each Newsstand app represents a magazine or newspaper; issues then appear within it.**

# Podcasts

**Cyber-shows** Podcasts are like radio or TV shows, but made for the internet. There are loads of free indie and professional podcasts available, and Apple's Podcasts app lets you find, subscribe and listen to them.

Tap Featured, Top Charts or Search at the bottom. You can choose whether audio or video podcasts are shown. Audio podcasts can be left playing while you use other apps; video can't.

You can download individual episodes or subscribe to get future ones automatically. Tap My Podcasts, and on each podcast's page, swipe downwards and tap Settings to manage that subscription, the order in which episodes are played, and whether they are retained or deleted afterwards.

My Stations lets you make auto-updating playlists to play episodes back to back.

↑ **All iTunes podcasts are free. You can subscribe to get future episodes automatically.**

# iTunes sync

**Desktop
to iPhone**

If you've bought music and movies from the iTunes Store on a Mac or PC, the best way to get them onto your iPhone is directly from Apple's servers, via More > Purchased in the iTunes Store app. But if you prefer to transfer files from the computer to your iPhone, you can do so. Unlike some mobile devices, your iPhone won't show its storage in the Mac's Finder or in Windows Explorer like a memory card and let you drag media files on and off it. Instead, you need to have your media in Apple's iTunes app in OS X or Windows and sync it from there to your iPhone.

The first time you sync your iPhone with iTunes on a Mac or PC (we'll show it on a Mac), you'll need to connect the iPhone to the computer using the iPhone's USB cable. The iPhone should then appear as a button at the top left of iTunes ❶ (older versions of iTunes vary). Click this, then click Summary in the sidebar. Under Options, tick 'Sync with this iPhone over Wi-Fi' ❷. In future, the iPhone button will appear in the iTunes app whenever your iPhone is connected to mains power and to the same wifi network as your Mac. You won't need to use the USB cable.

At the foot of the screen is a coloured graph ❸ showing what's on your iPhone and how much space is free. From the sidebar items labelled Apps, Music, Movies and so on ❹, you can pick which items will be

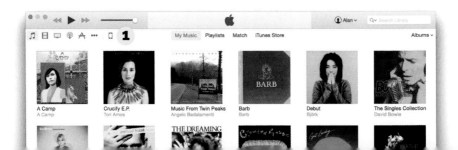

synced to your iPhone and see how the graph changes to reflect these choices. Nothing actually happens until you click Sync. When you do, the selected content will *replace* everything on your iPhone. Music and videos already on the iPhone but not set to sync from your Mac will be *erased*.

Alternatively, tick 'Manually manage music and videos' ❺. (Notice that on our screen, music isn't mentioned in this option: that's because we're using iTunes Match, which means we've opted to sync all our music from the cloud, not from our computer.) Then, when viewing your iTunes Library, drag any playlist, song or video onto the iPhone's pop-up sidebar.

If you want to transfer content *from* the iPhone *to* the Mac, go to iTunes' File menu and pick Devices > Transfer Purchases.

# iCloud sync

**Always there**

Setting up an iCloud account is one of the first things you'll do on your new iPhone, if you haven't previously. It brings many benefits, including the ability to sync data from various apps and services between all your devices – not just other iOS products, such as an iPad or iPod touch, but any Macs and Windows PCs you own as well.

The synced data isn't transferred directly between your devices and computers. Instead, it's automatically uploaded to Apple's servers whenever a device on which you've made changes to it has a connection to the internet, and your other devices automatically download it from there.

Open the Settings app and tap iCloud to see a list of the features that are supported. It includes calendar events, reminders, notes, bookmarks from iOS's Safari web browser, and documents in Apple's iWork apps (see p128). You can also track devices connected to your iCloud account – including your iPhone – using the Find My iPhone feature.

If you have a Mac, open System Preferences, click the iCloud icon and sign in with your Apple ID. You'll see a similar list of apps and services to the one on your iPhone, although some might be missing: Keychain, for example, if you're running version 10.8 or earlier of OS X, and Photos (which gives access to your iCloud Photo Library – see p120) if you don't have iPhoto, Aperture or their successor, the Photos app, on your Mac.

Ensure every item you want to keep in sync between your Mac and iPhone is ticked. The Keychain item syncs any website logins and bank card details you've asked Safari to record so that it can automatically fill out online forms. For bank cards, the long card number, the card holder's name and the start and expiry dates are stored, but not the security code

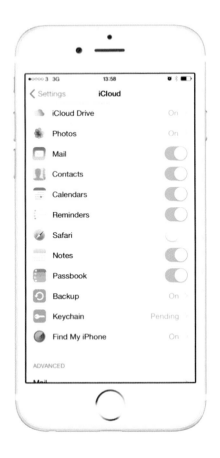

**← iCloud lets your iPhone, other Apple devices, Macs and PCs share a lot of everyday information, kept in sync automatically between them all.**

from the back of the card, which retailers should require from you when purchasing as an extra form of security. (You can manage what information is stored in Settings > Safari > Passwords & AutoFill.)

Turning on Keychain syncing involves some extra steps. You're asked to set a passcode, which will then need to be entered on any subsequent device that signs in to your iCloud account and tries to retrieve your Keychain. Giving the passcode proves it's you making the request. If you opt not to use a passcode, you'll need an already authorised device physically at hand whenever you want to allow Keychain syncing to a new one.

If you have a PC, iCloud syncing isn't built into Windows, but you can download Apple's iCloud Control Panel from support.apple.com/kb/dl1455. Fewer things sync to Windows, but calendars, contacts, mail and task lists in Microsoft Outlook are linked to their iCloud equivalents. The Control Panel can automatically download your iCloud photos, and it can sync bookmarks with Internet Explorer, Firefox or Google Chrome.

Some iCloud data can be viewed and edited directly from Apple's servers by logging in to icloud.com from a web browser on a Mac or PC. This isn't the way it's designed to be accessed from iOS, so if you go to icloud.com on your iPhone, you'll just see some setup options instead.

# Photo Library

**Pictures every-where**

The idea behind iCloud Photo Library is that every picture that arrives on any of your Apple devices (iOS or Mac), whether from its own camera or imported, is automatically uploaded to iCloud, at full quality, and becomes accessible from your other Apple devices. To turn it on, go to Settings > iCloud > Photos on your iPhone and flick the iCloud Photo Library switch. You'll be warned any photos currently synced to your phone from iTunes on a Mac or PC will be removed; this doesn't affect other photos. If you proceed, you can choose 'Download and Keep Originals' to keep photos at full quality on your iPhone *and* in iCloud. Alternatively, Optimise iPhone Storage only keeps a copy on your phone that's as big as its screen, saving storage space.

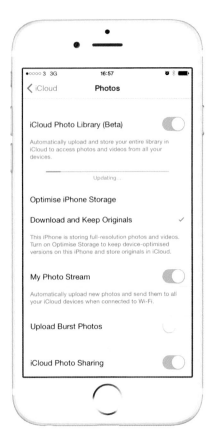

**↑ The beta version's warning to make a separate backup is always good practice anyway.**

**↗ The old Photo Stream and Photo Sharing services remain available for the moment too.**

**← Photo Library works across iOS devices running iOS 8 and Macs running OS X Yosemite.**

iCloud Photo Library may not be an infallible archive, so if you use it, be sure to keep a permanent copy of your photos elsewhere. If you're not offered a tutorial on this when you turn it on, see support.apple.com/kb/ht4083. At the time of writing, the Photos app is due to replace iPhoto on the Mac, and will become the main route to backing up your pictures.

# Family Sharing

**Together at last**

If you're a multi-device household, it's likely you each have your own Apple ID to make purchases from the iTunes Store and App Store. Until iOS 8, this left you with a problem with sharing media and apps among family members: you have to either authorise all their devices to play content bought from each others' accounts, or all share the same account, which can cause numerous problems. That's why iOS 8 includes a new option called Family Sharing.

This feature allows up to six accounts to be identified as part of the same family. Once done, each member's purchases are available to the others through the Store apps to download just as easily as those items purchased using their own account.

This depends on everyone's account being connected to the same bank card. Your kids' accounts can be set to require your approval before any purchase,

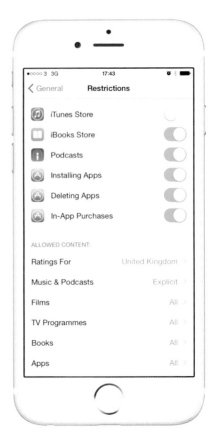

**← A family has one Organiser, but you can identify another as a parent to supervise spending.**

**↑ When your child wants to buy something, a notification will ask for your permission.**

**↗ Complement this by using iOS's Restrictions as parental controls (see p68).**

which means you'll receive a message requesting a yes or no.

Everyone can also contribute to the same photo album and share a common calendar.

To set up Family Sharing, start on a device that's signed in to the iCloud account that will be the Family Organiser. Go to Settings > iCloud, tap Family Sharing and follow the prompts.

# Chapter 5
# **Apps**

# iMovie

**Lights! iPhone! Action!**

Videos that you've recorded with your iPhone can be viewed in the Photos app, which also enables you to trim a clip and share it online. But Apple also provides the iMovie app with every new iPhone, bringing you more advanced tools to create polished HD videos without using a Mac. iMovie's excellent use of gestures makes it quick and easy to edit videos ❶, even on a small screen. Pinching or spreading apart two fingers zooms in or out of the timeline. Swiping down through a clip cuts it in two. Swiping up creates a freeze-frame. iMovie comes with several themes, including Bright, Travel and News, which provide high-impact motion graphics and musical scores to add to your video. iMovie is also a good way to make more interesting slideshows from your still photos by applying 'Ken Burns'–style dynamic effects to them.

# GarageBand

**The music in you**

There's no better illustration of the iPhone's scope as a creative tool. GarageBand turns your phone into a realistic guitar, drum kit, piano and even string orchestra, all played on the screen. You can lay down vocals with the iPhone's mic, add effects, and turn any recorded sound into a keyboard instrument. GarageBand mimics how real instruments look ❷ and, roughly, how they work. Smart Instruments simplify things by automating the playing of chords and rhythms, but leaving you enough control to make the music your own. A MIDI keyboard can be connected with an adaptor. Guitar input can be processed like an effects pedal.

The app is great for noodling around, but you can be ambitious and lay down multiple tracks, edit notes in the Tracks view, and mix your songs. The built-in Loops are great for making iMovie soundtracks, too.

# iWork

**Office in your pocket**

Pages, Numbers and Keynote are the three components of Apple's office suite – although 'office' doesn't do justice to a set of apps that's also incredibly useful at home, for writing letters and laying out documents, keeping track of your budget, doing homework and making slide-shows. Each app costs a few pounds, but they're free with a new iPhone.

These apps integrate with iCloud, and the first time you open each one, they'll ask if you want to use iCloud Drive to store your documents (see p132). If you accept this, any changes you make in this app on your iPhone are synced to your other devices ready for the next time you use the same app. The Mac versions of the three iWork apps also sync: the same documents can be edited seamlessly on desktop or mobile.

If you don't have the apps on your Mac, or use a PC (iWork isn't available for Windows), you can edit your documents in a web browser. Log in at icloud.com on your computer and click the Pages, Numbers or Keynote icon to view and edit the documents you created on your iPhone.

In the iOS apps, you can format text in Pages, add formulae to Numbers spreadsheets, and use media from the Photos and Music apps in Keynote presentations, which are much more stylish than PowerPoint. After all, this is the app that was created for Steve Jobs' Apple keynotes.

The iWork apps are more fully usable on an iPad or Mac, but even on your phone you can at least get documents started, and the iPhone 6 Plus's bigger screen makes things a bit less cramped. The apps are fast and responsive, and gestures let you carry out complex operations easily.

If you still find the small touchscreen uncomfortably fiddly for typing, reading and formatting, there are a couple of things you can add

to your iPhone. Pairing any Bluetooth keyboard (the Apple Wireless Keyboard supplied with Macs works fine) makes long-form text entry more practical. And an Apple TV or Digital AV Adaptor plus an HDMI cable connected to a TV set will give you a full-size display. The TVs in hotel rooms sometimes have accessible HDMI ports, incidentally.

All three apps present your documents as thumbnails in a grid **❶**. You can group documents in folders, and starting with iOS 8, iCloud finally lets you store documents from different apps in the same folder (and to nest one folder inside another to organise them). Tap to open a folder, then tap its name to amend it. Pull down at the top of the list to reveal options to sort by date or name. Tap a document to open it, or

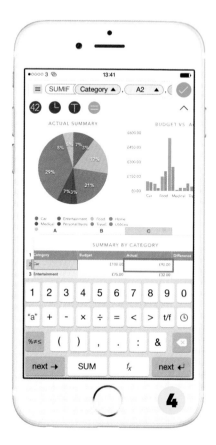

tap '+' to create a new one. The latter will show a selection of templates ❷, including CVs, letters and invitations in Pages; a budget planner, savings tracker and exercise log in Numbers; and presentations in Keynote.

Use the same pinch and swipe gestures as in Safari to zoom into and pan around your documents. Type over the placeholder text with your own. Formatting can be copied from one bit of text to another: double-tap a word in the style you want to replicate ❸, tap the Style item and choose Copy Style. Double-tap a word in the block you want to restyle, drag the text selection markers to encompass the whole block, select Style and pick Paste Style. Tap once in your document with no text selected and choose Insert from the menu to add tabs, page breaks, column breaks and more.

Double-tap a cell in Numbers to reveal the keypad ❹. The items under the green top bar define what you'll put into it; the keypad changes accordingly. Tap '=' to enter a formula. Type 'SUM' on the keyboard and a region of cells is marked in the document; drag its handles to select the range of data to add up, or drag its centre to move the selection around.

Keynote comes with plenty of templates to start you off. Tap an item on any slide ❺ and choose Animate to decide how it'll appear and disappear ❻. Tap '+' at the top to add media, tables, charts and shapes. Tap a chart and choose Edit Data to tailor it as you like.

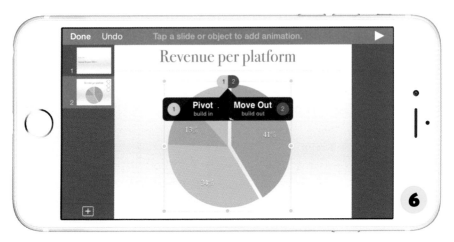

# iCloud Drive

**A bright forecast**

Apps can store documents and other data in iCloud (meaning on Apple's remote servers). They've been able to do this for some time, but the oversimplified way it worked in the past, segregating each app's files, is replaced in iOS 8 and OS X Yosemite by iCloud Drive. This works like a disk or memory stick. Although each app gets a special folder in which to save things, you can add folders to organise things however you want.

If you've had your iCloud account for a while, you'll still have the old 'Documents in the Cloud' system until you tell iCloud to upgrade it to iCloud Drive. You can do that via Settings > iCloud > iCloud Drive.

**→ Apps that save to Cloud Drive present it the same way using this document picker.**

**↙ iCloud Drive keeps documents in sync on iOS devices, Macs and Windows PCs.**

Apps that can save to iCloud Drive all present it in the same way: a grid of file and folder icons, which can be switched to a list. Pull downwards to find options to sort the contents by name, date modified and attached tags.

in Settings > iCloud > iCloud Drive, you can choose which apps are allowed to save to Drive (you

get 5GB of space free; to buy more, see support.apple.com/kb/ht4874) or only to local storage.

Whatever's in your Drive is kept in sync between any iPhone, iPad or iPod touch running iOS 8 and Macs running OS X 10.10 Yosemite. On Macs, iCloud Drive's contents are viewed and managed through the Finder, just like a physical external drive.

# Handoff

**Team players**

Sometimes you'll start to write an email, read a lengthy web page or view a presentation on your iPhone, then decide you'd get through it faster on your Mac. Handoff lets you do this with no effort at all, as long as your Mac is running OS X Yosemite and has Bluetooth 4.0 built in. Your iPhone and Mac will need to be signed into the same iCloud account.

When the two devices are near each other, an app icon automatically appears at the left of the Mac's Dock. This says the Mac recognises you're doing something on the iPhone that it can take over. It doesn't work with all apps, but with many of those from Apple, and other devel-

**↑ Look to the bottom left of the Lock screen to carry on a task you started on your Mac.**

**↗ Handoff signals its availability in the App Switcher if your iPhone is already unlocked.**

**← Handoff works with many Apple apps, but only in iOS 8, and OS X Yosemite on the Mac.**

opers can add this ability to their Mac and iOS apps too.

Handoff also works the other way, so if you don't finish something before you have to go out, a swipe is all it takes to prepare your iPhone to continue it on the way home. (You will need to do that before leaving, though.) It makes using several Apple devices all the more convenient.

# Games

In sheer numbers, iOS is the world's biggest games platform. The iPhone is ideal for casual gaming, especially with the App Store offering instant downloads. But the iPhone is also home to heavyweight racing, sports and combat titles and innovative platform, arcade and adventure games. Apple's use of increasingly powerful processors, with particularly impressive 3D graphics capabilities, shows it's serious about offering 'console quality'.

Browse the Games section in the App Store app to see the variety available. External reviews on gaming websites and in magazines will help you find the best titles. When a game is listed as 'free', tap for its description and scroll down to 'In-App Purchases': you'll often find there's plenty to spend money on. In some cases a small one-off payment gets you the full game; in others, cash buys power-ups or 'coins' without which your progress is slowed. These purchases are made by entering your Apple ID password

or using Touch ID within the game. Titles with no IAP are truly free.

You'll always be told when you're being charged, but less experienced users may overlook this, and some games are designed to encourage you to keep paying. If you're concerned, you can turn off In-App Purchases via Restrictions (p68) or use Family Sharing (p122) to control other users' purchasing.

**↑ Asphalt 8 makes use of the iPhone's accelerometer to let you steer by tilting the device, using buttons on the touchscreen to control your speed.**

**← Apple's Game Center connects you with other iOS gamers and facilitates online play as well as keeping track of your progress and scores.**

**Game Center**

Even casual games have high scores to beat and personal bests to better. To keep data like this stored safely, along with level and character progress, and available to different devices you might have the same game installed on, Apple provides Game Center, a cloud for games. It also facilitates sharing and multiplayer, and has its own app of the same name where you can see details of your gaming activity. You'll know when a game uses Game Center because a message saying 'Welcome back,' with the Game Center logo, pops up to greet you each time you play it.

# Chapter 6
# Accessories

# Cables and cases

**⬇ Lightning to Digital AV**
This adaptor from Apple sends video and audio from your iPhone via HDMI to HDTV sets and digital projectors.

**⬅ microUSB adaptor**
Connects your iPhone to a standard mobile phone charging cable.

**⬇ Lightning to 30-pin**
This one-piece adaptor, also available as a cable (see opposite page), connects your iPhone 6 to most accessories made for the older iOS port. Video isn't supported.

**➡ Lightning to VGA**
For older equipment, this adaptor outputs an analogue video signal from your iPhone. You'll need a standard VGA cable too, and audio will have to go by another route, such as the headphone socket.

## Apple iPhone 6 covers

There are hundreds of other iPhone 6 cases to choose from, but Apple's leather case is neatly made and comes in a range of tasteful colours. It wraps around the front edge to protect the beautifully curved glass, and provides openings for all the ports and switches as well as the rear camera and flash. The alternative silicone case works the same way, but with a soft matt finish.

**↑ Lightning to 30-pin cable**

Apple's cases are completely open at the bottom edge, but if you use a third-party case that just has a cutout for the Lightning port, any adaptors you buy will need to be the cable type, or they won't fit.

## Cygnett
# AeroGrip

One complaint about the iPhone 6 is that its polished surfaces and round edges make it easy to drop. The AeroGrip fixes that. Available in black, white or crystal clear, it gives you a secure hold on your 6 or 6 Plus.

**£9.95** from amazon.co.uk. See uk.cygnett.com for details

## iChic Gear
# Little Marcel Folio

Chic by name, chic by nature – the Little Marcel must be one of the most stylish statements for your iPhone 6. The folio incorporates a rubberised hard case for all-round protection and a front flap to safeguard the screen. All ports and the rear camera remain accessible.  Also available in alternative designs and as a hard case or sock.

**€30.90** (about £24) including delivery to UK from ichicgear.com

## TwelveSouth
# HiRise

TwelveSouth makes some of the most beautiful Apple accessories, and the HiRise is no exception. It's highly practical, too. The brushed metal pedestal holds your iPhone up where you can see it, whether for FaceTime or just to keep an eye on social media. The ports are left clear, so you can plug in your Lightning charger and use your EarPods or the built-in speaker without encumbrance.

**£29.95** from store.apple.com/uk. See twelvesouth.com for details

# Braven
## 705

The iPhone 6's built-in speaker is decent, but it can't do justice to the audio available from iTunes music and HD movies. The splashproof eight-inch Braven 705 connects via cable or Bluetooth wireless and provides rich sound with solid bass. A noise-cancelling mic is built in for hands-free calls, and you can top up your iPhone from its rechargeable battery. Available in eight colours.

**£89.95** from braven.eu/stores

# Christian Lacroix
## 'Butterflies' Cover

Available in a range of colours including subtle black, this unique iPhone 6
cover features a polyurethane textile
finish over a resin hard case. The signa-
ture Christian Lacroix butterfly shadow
design brings brilliant colours to your
phone while helping to protect it from
everyday bumps and knocks.

**£17** from amazon.co.uk
See bigben-interactive.co.uk
for details

# Native Union
## Jump

This zebra-striped nylon braided
USB charging cable, suitable
for all iPhones with a Lightning
port, will keep you talking on the
move. When you have access
to power, connect the USB plug
on the reverse of the unit; when
you don't, top up your charge
from the handy built-in battery.

**£39.99** from
nativeunion.com/uk

THE INDEPENDENT GUIDE
TO THE

# iPhone 6 and 6 Plus

**Editor in Chief and Creative Director**
Adam Banks for Vast Landscape Ltd

**Senior Writer**
Alan Stonebridge

### MANAGEMENT

**Group Publisher**
Paul Rayner
paul_rayner@dennis.co.uk

**Group Advertising Manager**
Alex Skinner
alex_skinner@dennis.co.uk

**MagBook Publisher** Dharmesh Mistry

**Newstrade Director** David Barker
**Operations Director** Robin Ryan
**MD of Advertising** Julian Lloyd-Evans
**MD of Enterprise** Martin Belson
**Chief Operating Officer** Brett Reynolds
**Group Finance Director** Ian Leggett
**Chief Executive** James Tye
**Company Founder** Felix Dennis

**Licensing and Syndication**
To license this product, please contact
Carlotta Serantoni on +44 (0) 20 7907
6550 or email carlotta_serantoni@
dennis.co.uk. To syndicate content from
this product, please contact Anj Dosaj-
Halai on +44(0) 20 7907 6132 or email
anj_dosaj-halai@dennis.co.uk

**Liability**
While every care was taken during
the production of this MagBook, the
publishers cannot be held responsible
for the accuracy of the information
or any consequence arising from it.

MacUser